REVEALING

OF THE SONS OF GOD

JOYCELYN OGUNSOLA

ISBN-13: 978-0692740767
ISBN- 10: 0692740767

Romans 8:19

"For the earnest expectation of creation eagerly waits for the revealing of the sons of God."

DEDICATION

To my parents,

Omotayo & Marcellinah

Thank you for instilling in me the principles of Christ since birth.

I love you both very much and I promise to make you both proud!

To my siblings,

Patrick, Felicia & Joshua

Y'all know if one makes it we all make it right?

Shoot for the stars and you can accomplish anything!

I love you guys!

And to The Lover of My Soul and the King of my Heart,

Jesus Christ...

On December 28th, 2011 you brought me into your Kingdom

and you changed my name.

And for that, I am forever indebted to you.

May my life forever bring glory to your name. I look forward to

dancing with you in eternity!

REVEALING OF THE SONS OF GOD

REVEALING OF THE SONS OF GOD

Table of Contents

Acknowledgments

"Will God ever ask you to do something you are not able to do? The answer is yes-all the time! It must be that way, for God's glory and kingdom. If we function according to our ability alone, we get the glory; if we function according to the power of the Spirit within us, God gets the glory."
-Henry T. Blackbay

With that being said, even if I wanted to take the credit for this work, I couldn't because I recognize that the inspiration behind this book came from the Holy Spirit. This work is not something that I could have possibly came up with on my own. So I acknowledge my helper and my divine inspiration—Holy Spirit who is completely and 100% behind the writing of this book.

"Not unto us, O Lord not unto us, but to Your name be the glory, because of your love and your faithfulness."
-Psalm 115:1

And to everyone who has helped me throughout the entire process of the publication of this work — whether it be financially or spiritually, I say thank you.

Your support and love means the world to me and it surely does not go unnoticed. I pray that the Lord God Almighty will bless you, keep you, make His face to shine upon you and continue to be gracious unto you.

INTRODUCTION

We've been looking for answers and searching for change in all the wrong places. Many of us are even questioning God's sovereignty and wondering where He is and what He's doing in the midst of all the crisis that the world brings. Questions like, *"If God is real then why doesn't He just stop all of this?"* and *"If God is truly a loving God then why do we have so much hate in world?"* tend to probe our thoughts and minds.

But I tell you that God is not silent! He is looking down from His throne room in Heaven and sees all that is going on in this world right now.

And what is His answer?

Many Sons being just like The Firstborn Son.

For hundreds and hundreds of years there have been children of God but this generation is destined to reach a point of maturation and become Sons of God.

Wherever you are, as you are reading this book, I pray that the eyes of your heart will be enlightened to know the hope of your calling and that is… to be a Son of God.

1

BACK TO THE BEGINNING

Genesis 1:1 "In the beginning..." (NLT)

Everything in life has a beginning.

A flower begins as a seed, a butterfly begins as a caterpillar, and this book began with an introduction! And just as these, we too have a beginning! We start off as a divine thought in God's mind, then from there we move on to conception; and from conception we are birthed into this world and begin developing—from infancy to toddlers, to school-age children, to adolescence and from adolescence into adulthood. With every new stage of our lives we just continue growing and maturing!

Everything that was ever created has both a beginning and an end. But what makes the beginning stages of anything in life so important is the foundation. The foundation is the infrastructure; it's the groundwork, it's the basis of everything. When an architecture and his team wants to create a building, the first thing they have to do is lay a foundation for the building because the foundation is what shapes and determines what the building will eventually look like and become. In the same way, before God created you, He had to lay down a foundation for your life. This foundation was not only *laid* but *slain* before time even began and his name is Jesus Christ.

Before you were born God already had your whole life all planned out. Not only did He make provision for a Savior but He made a foundation (which is the support). And Jesus is your life-support. He is the one who ultimately shapes and determines who you are and who you will someday become. He is the groundwork, He is the infrastructure, and He is the basis of your whole entire life.1st Corinthians 3:11 says, *"For no one can lay any foundation other than the one we already have—Jesus Christ."*

The foundation that was laid for you at the beginning of your life is Jesus Christ. And because this foundation was laid this means that every other foundation is futile. Every other infrastructure is pointless because no other foundation can be laid other than Him. No other person gets a say in who you are except him because He is the only one knew you before you were born.

Without the foundation (Jesus Christ) being established at the beginning there would be no proof of your existence. There would not even be a beginning to look back on or to revisit.

WHERE IDENTITY & PURPOSE COLLIDE

The beginning is where everything was first given its identity and purpose. We see this in Jeremiah 1:5 when God speaks directly to Jeremiah's identity and says, *"Before I formed you in the womb I knew you; before you were born I sanctified you; I ordained you as a prophet to the nations."*

In order for you to mature into the fullness of all that God has called and created you to be the first thing you need to know is who you are. Before Jeremiah could go out and be a prophet to the nations, God made sure that He got Jeremiah's attention, pulled him to the side and said... *"Look, before you were even born I knew who you were. I loved you. I cherished you. I cared for you and you are my son."* God spoke to directly to his identity.

Ephesians 1:3-4 says:

"For He chose us in Him before the foundation of the world to be holy and blameless in His presence. In love, He predestined us for adoption as His sons through Jesus Christ, according to the good pleasure of

His will."

Way before the beginning even began, you were chosen by God to be a Son. But not just *a* Son—*His* Son. And in love, you were predestined to be conformed into the image of The Firstborn Son, Jesus Christ (Romans 8:29). You are destined to be an image-bearer of Jesus Christ. Your life was already predetermined for you way before your mother and father even crossed paths with each other. You didn't choose this life that you live, God chose it for you. Your existence is according to the good pleasure of His will. God willed that your birth would happen and so it did and now you're here! To *"will"* something means to have a personal choice or desire, and it was God's personal desire for you to be born to the parents that you have, to have the nationality that you are and live in the country that you are living in.

It's His will, His choice and His desire. God is the one who is behind your birth. He is the only one who has a legalistic right and gets a say in who you are. If God says that you are loved then no one can speak against that. If God says that you have purpose then no one can counteract that truth. No one can speak against your identity. No one gets to call you out of your name. Not your parents, friends, or even yourself. If God said it then who can stand against what He has already spoken? The answer is nobody. Nobody is that powerful. God's word will never return back to Him void and what He says about you is true and final. When someone calls you out of your name, speaks wrongfully against your identity and purpose then they have just done something illegal. They have just messed with a Kingdom citizen.

Never again do you have to listen to the opinion of men. You are not who your parents say you are. You are not who your friends and colleagues say you are. You are not even what you say you are. You are who God says you are. Allow yourself to be free from the opinion of man and allow this simple yet profound truth to permeate your whole being.

Today, many of people are in search

of who they are. Everything inside of man is aching to discover our identity so we look to different means such as joining clubs and organizations, getting involved in different relationships, hanging out with the wrong crowd and even believing the lies that people have told us. We are literally looking everywhere in this hopeless world to discover who we are. But Romans 5:5 says that *" true hope doesn't disappoint!"* This should let you know that you're looking in the wrong place.

Who you are is not inside this world, it's deep inside of you. Your identity cannot escape you; it's in you, but sin is what's keeping it hidden. Hidden deep inside of our beings are our truest selves but we don't know it because it has yet to be awakened to us.

Your identity is not this farfetched thing. It's not something that is so out of reach for you. Although your identity may seem like an unsolved mystery to you, it is surely no mystery to God. You don't have to tread through life trying to find your identity because your identity was placed inside of you at the beginning and an awakening needs to happen in your spirit in order for it to be rediscovered.

The first thing to do in order for you to get to a place of this "Great Awakening" is by taking a trip back to the beginning.

Why the beginning you ask? Because, the beginning is where you find God's original intent and purpose for your life.

But not just for your life, for all of creation too.

THE BEGINNING

The beginning is where life was given. The beginning is where God created all things out of nothing and we see how He did so in such an orderly and strategic way. It is where He spoke and things came into existence. No wonder why John 1:3 says, *"All things were made through Him, and without Him nothing was made that was made."* It is where the sun, moon and the stars were created, it's where the earth and the seas were created, and it is where the solar systems, planets and different seasons were created. Day and Night were created in the beginning. The sea creatures, land creatures and all of the birds of the air were all created in the beginning. After God finished creating all of these creatures, Genesis 1:22 says, *"And God blessed them, saying, "Be fruitful and multiply, and fill the waters in the seas, and let birds multiply the earth."* Right after God created these creatures He didn't just leave them without any work, He gave them purpose!

In Genesis Chapter 1 we see how God takes a huge mass of complete nothingness and with tremendous order, variety, and beauty creates all of things out of nothing. Step by step, God strategically called forth creation through the power of His Word. He begins with calling forth the grand things such as: light, day and night, the earth and the waters. Then, He effortlessly works His way to the more particular things like plants and animals and then He finally ends with creating man. (I believe that this is where the phrase, *'save the best for last'* came from!)

If you read closely, scripture says in Genesis 1 that each time after God had finished creating something, He looked at it and, *"He saw that it was good."* But wait, this wasn't the case for man! In fact, Genesis 1: 26-31 tells us that after God created man on the Sixth Day of the Creation week, He had a little something different to say.

" *26 Then God said, "Let Us make man in Our image, according to Our likeness; let them have dominion over the fish of the sea, over the birds of the air, and over the cattle, over all the earth and over every creeping thing that creeps on the earth." 27 So God created man in His own image; in the image of God He created him; male and female He created them. 28 Then God blessed them, and God said to them, "Be fruitful and multiply; fill the earth and subdue it; have dominion over the fish of the sea, over the birds of the air, and over every living thing that moves on the earth."29 And God said, "See, I have given you every herb that yields seed which is on the face of all the earth, and every tree whose fruit yields seed; to you it shall be for food. 30 Also, to every beast of the earth, to every bird of the air, and to everything that creeps on the earth, in which there is life, I have given every green herb for food"; and it was so.* [31] *Then God saw everything that He had made, and indeed it was very good. So the evening and the morning were the sixth day.* (NKJV)

These scriptures actually hit a couple key points that I want to lay emphasis on:

1. Man was created in the image and likeness of the Godhead. (Verse 27)
2. Man was given dominion (or reign) over everything that God created except each other. (Verse 28)
3. It wasn't until after God created man that He looked at everything He had made and saw that it indeed was very good. (Verse 31)

There is just something about going back to the beginning that opens your eyes and allows you to realize your identity, your purpose and why you were created. These three points are very important because they express the importance of man and speak so much about our identity as sons.

The first point I made was that man was created in the image and likeness of The

Godhead —God the Father, God the Son and God the Holy Spirit. Meaning that we were created to be just like God. Not to be Him, but to be *like Him*. He gave us characteristics that reflect His nature. And in a sense, we are "little gods". Scripture even makes it clear and says in Psalm 82:6 (NIV), *"You are "gods"; you are all sons of the Most High."* Notice how in this scripture, David puts the letter 'g" in "gods" in lowercase because he was referring to man — the Sons of God, not God Himself.

We were not created to be God because God is a God all by Himself and He does not need anyone contending with His supremacy. God is big enough to reign all by Himself. But remember Lucifer's rebellion? He thought he was so beautiful, so intelligent and so powerful in the position that God bestowed upon him that he actually desired for himself the glory that was only deserving of God alone. Although God created Lucifer with all these angelic characteristics to be like Him and to reflect His glory, he rebelled against God and because of the pride of his sin, he wanted to be God.

In Ephesians 5:1, Paul tells us to be imitators of God. To walk like Him, love like Him, think like Him; speak like Him and to move in power and authority and dominion just like Him. And because He created us in His likeness, this is where we get our identity from. I want you to read this like it's really true. This verse is very profound but so commonly overlooked and it's why many people (including believers) don't know who they are.

God wanted to fill the earth with His nature and He chose to do so through His Sons. Why? Because out of everything that He created, He wanted to create something that would look like Him— something that would be a representative of Him on earth. Something that would exude the exact characteristics of His Spirit which are: love, joy, peace, patience, kindness, goodness, faithfulness, gentleness and self control. God wanted to create something that would be an image-bearer of His glory so He put it in a dirt suit and called it man. Man was the only thing that God created in the image and likeness of Himself. That right there should automatically make you feel special because that means nothing else in all of creation can compare or even contend with you because you embody the very characteristics and nature of God.

You look like God. Allow that to resonate within you. You look Him. Not the angels in Heaven, but you. You look exactly like your Father in Heaven! The Bible even gives us a clear image of what God looks like in Revelations 1:14-15 when it says, *"His head and hair are white like wool, as white as snow, and His eyes like a flame of fire; His feet were like fine brass, as if refined in a furnace, and His voice as the sound of many waters."* God has hair, eyes, feet, voice, hands, fingers, ears and etc. Now of course, no human being has feet like fine brass, or eyes like the flames of fire. But these different body parts originated from God. The scientist may have named them, but God created them. God gave us these different physical traits because he wanted us to look like Him. You may see some people who have brown hair and some who have blonde.

But they still have hair just as like God. Some people may have hazel brown eyes while others may have blue. But they still have eyes just like God as well. Psalm 8:5 says *"You have made them a little lower than the angels and crowned them with glory and honor."* This scripture is talking about man. God has bestowed unto each of us our own glory that's why all of us are different. Different; but all made in His image and likeness.

In my second point, I key in on how God gave His Sons dominion and reign over everything except each other. After creating us in His image and likeness I can imagine Him saying, "In order for you to effectively be like me in this world, you have to possess some of my traits." God possesses many idiosyncrasies, but on this Sixth day, He goes on ahead and gives His Sons dominion over everything that He has created. God knew that in order for us to operate in this world like Him we had to have some amount of power. Scripture says that He has given us everything we need to be just like Him in this life. (2nd Peter 1:3 *"By his divine power, God has given us everything we need for living a godly life.")*

God gave His Sons dominion over earth to lead, to rule, to reign, to manage, to govern and to protect it. Many of us think that we have to be in an appointed position before we can act as leaders when we in fact were all born to lead. We are all created to lead in a certain area of gifting. Leadership is not just for the pastors, the government politicians, the governors, the mayors, it's for the Sons! In fact, it was meant for the Sons but because of a lack of not knowing who we are, it has caused us to deem ourselves as powerless, when in fact this is not true.

We have lost sight of what God has placed us on this earth to do. This is why it's important for us to revisit the beginning so that we can re-gain knowledge of our mandate here on earth and begin to confidently walk in all that God has called us to be.

The last point that I want to lay emphasis on is that God had something different to say after He finished creating man. It wasn't until after God created us and gave us dominion over the earth that *"He looked over all he had made, and he saw that it was very good!"* (Genesis 1:31) Everything that God had created prior to the creation of man—the sky, the waters, the birds, vegetation and everything else—was good. But the use of the word *"very"* in Genesis 1:31 implies that man represented God's crowning achievement of creating the world.

Every day, God commanded each event to happen by saying *"Let there be"* and the moment the sound of His voice released an echo into the universe, the command that he spoke came into existence! But when it came down to the creation of man, there was a difference because on that Sixth day, God did not command, He consulted. He called forth the Godhead and said come, *"Let Us, make man in our own image."* God in all of his sovereignty could have easily commanded the creation of man just as He did with the animals and all of life's vegetation but instead, He chose not to. I believe that God had it this way so that it could be made clear that man is in no way, in any close relations with animals or plants. But rather, that man is someone different; someone marvelous, the most excellent of all of God's creation and His exact handiwork created to do good works in this world!

Although man was formed from dust, Genesis 2:7 says, *"God breathed into his nostrils the breath of life; and man became a living being."* This scripture makes it clear that man's life wasn't by happenstance nor was it derived from evolution (like the scientists suggest). But man was literally handcrafted by God and is a gift from God.

Genesis 5:1-2 emphasis's this when explaining the genealogy of Adam, *"This is the book of the genealogy of Adam. In the day that God created man. He made him in the likeness of God. He created them male and female, and blessed them and called them Mankind in the day they were created."* Adam wasn't taken from any form of animal; he was taken from God and made in the image and likeness of God.

It is crucial that you recognize how important the creation of mankind is because once you see God's intent and heart behind creating man; your heart will be open to receive your identity as a Son.

We must know who we are before we can effectively begin to walk into whom we are. Of course, in its entirety, all of God's creation is great. But mankind was (and still is) God's greatest creation of all. You need to know that you are one of God's greatest creations!

One of my favorite things to do in life is to watch the sunset. I mean, just by gazing it, I am fully convinced that there is indeed a God; And I am even more convinced that it has got to be the most beautiful of all of God's creation. Nevertheless, man is the summation of God's creation. After God finished creating that gorgeous sunset, He said *"it was good."* It wasn't until after He got done creating man, that He saw that *"it was very good."* This just goes to show that there has got to be something special about us. There has got to be something peculiar about us. There has got to be something inside of us that this world needs. And in fact, there is.

God's purpose behind creating man in His image and likeness was so that we could be just like Him (as stated earlier). Even though God is spirit and does not have a bodily form like that of a man, when He chooses to visibly appear before man, He does so in the form of a human body.

In the book, *The Genesis Record,* written by Christian apologist Dr. Henry Morris, Morris said, *"There is something about the human body therefore, which is uniquely appropriate to God's manifestation of Himself, and (since God knows all His works from the beginning of the world—Acts 15:18), He must have designed man's body with this in mind. Accordingly He designed it, not like the animals, but with an erect posture, with an upward gazing countenance, capable of facial expressions corresponding with emotional feelings, and with a brain and tongue capable of articulate, symbolic speech."*

I love how in Psalm 139:13-15 David acknowledges how wonderful his bodily form is. Here's what he had to say: *"You made all the delicate, inner parts of my body and knit me together in my mother's womb. Thank you for making me so wonderfully complex! Your workmanship is marvelous-how well I know it. You watched me as I was being formed in utter seclusion, as I was woven together in the dark of the womb."*(NLT)

I mean, come on! The Bible does not speak about any of God's creations in a manner such as this! This verse says that God knit us together in our mother's womb. The word '*knit*' means to join firmly or closely together. If you've ever seen someone such as your grandmother take a ball of yarn and actually knit a sweater, and watch them closely, you see that it requires a lot of patience, precision and great skill. This is exactly what our Maker did! He called forth the Godhead and together they (with great patience) took their time to knit you; to create you. I could just imagine them taking many different balls of yarn that each has different labels on them; one labeled *'love'*, the other *'painter'* and another labeled *'singer'*. They took all these different characteristics, talents, and gifts and skillfully and strategically worked together to create a beautiful you. And because every single human being is different and has a different genetic makeup, I imagine that the Godhead had to go through this process a billion different times! Geez! Imagine how much time that took!

HISTORY'S PAST

The beginning was a perfect time in history and one of the most significant times. However, it's a shame to say that this time in history (everything before Genesis 3) is the most ignored and overlooked subject in the Christian culture today. This ignorance of our origin deprives us of our sense of not knowing who we are as Sons of God. It also robs us of not knowing what our role is in the whole construction and re-construction of creation. It's no wonder why the Hosea 4:6 says, *"My people are destroyed because of a lack of knowledge."* Failure of not knowing who you are can result in destruction of your destiny.

Many people in this generation (and even in past generations) are struggling with different things spiritually and often times, don't even know why. One of the reasons may be because they have not gone back to the beginning. They have not traced their roots back to see if their ancestors practiced witchcraft, worshipped idols, offered up sacrifices to other gods or if they practiced any other form of sin. Many millennial's are suffering from the sins of their parent's and because of this they are kept in a spiritual bondage called generational curse.

A generational curse is a reoccurrence of a negative behavior or pattern of some sort that has been passed down from one generation to another in your family. Have you ever wondered why nobody in your family has graduated from college? Why every woman in your family has had a miscarriage? Or even why every member in your family has a serious anger problem? This is not some type of "learned behavior" like psychologists would say. This is a spiritual bondage that must be broken and the first step to receiving freedom is by first repenting. To repent means to turn away from something.

If you want to be all that God has called you to be, if you want to live a life full of purpose and destiny, if you want to walk in your identity as a Son of God, you must go back to the beginning. You must to get on your knees before the Lord and repent. Repent for all the sins that your father and your father's father have committed—not just for their sake but for yours. Your life is too precious and too valuable to be manipulated and truncated by the enemy. Remember, you were created in the image and likeness of God, meaning that you were born to *be like God,* not like your father who was a porn-addict, or like your mother who was an alcoholic. You need get on your knees, repent and claim what is rightfully yours as Son of God. Don't allow the enemy to have a foothold over your life.

According to Numbers 14:19 Moses did the same thing for the people of Israel, he repented on their behalf and said, "*Pardon the iniquity of this people, I pray, according to the greatness of Your mercy, just as You have forgiven this people, from Egypt even until now.*" Then the Lord answered his prayer and said, "*I have pardoned, according to your word.*" (Numbers 14:20 NKJV)

But before all of this, if you don't even know Jesus Christ as your Lord and Savior and don't have a genuine relationship with Him nothing else in this book will make sense to you because in order for you walk in the fullness of all that God has called you to be, the first step is knowing Him.

So I want to lead you in a prayer:

Dear Lord,

I acknowledge that I am sinner in need of grace. I believe in my heart and confess with my mouth that you sent your Son, Jesus Christ to pay a ransom for all my sins. I accept Him into my life, and I give Him permission to be Lord over my life. I receive my identity as a Son and I pray that you will give me the grace to walk in this. Help me to live a life that is pleasing to you, according to the good pleasure of your will.

In Jesus name I pray. Amen.

If you prayed this prayer with a sincere and genuine heart then congratulations, you have been saved!

-

Jesus came to earth already having the full revelation of who He was. When asked before the council of men in Luke 22:70. *'"Are you the Son of God?"* He replied saying, *"You rightly say that I am."* Throughout His life on earth, Jesus made statements like: "I AM THE RESURRECTION AND THE LIFE", "I AM THE BREAD OF HEAVEN", "I AM THE LIGHT THE WORLD," "I AM THE TRUE VINE". The only way that Jesus was able to boldly profess statements such as these (even while people were speaking against His identity) is because He knew who He was and who He came from. In order for us to reign as a Sons of God, we to must have a revelation of who we are and an understanding of where we come from because this will ultimately govern the way we perceive ourselves.

BACK TO THE KINGDOM

Visiting the beginning stages opens our eyes and gives us insight and revelation on what God's intent for man was and that was to be representatives of the Kingdom of Heaven on earth. We were sent here from the beginning of creation to bring the Kingdom of Heaven to earth. Earth is supposed to be exactly like Heaven under the ruler ship of God's Sons! We see this in Isaiah 45: 18 which says, *"For the LORD is God and he created the heavens and earth and put everything in place. He made the world to be lived in, not to be a place of empty chaos. "I am the LORD," he says, "and there is no other."* I love how this version says, "He made the world to be lived in, not to be a place of empty chaos." The Greek word for 'live' is *Zao* and it means *'life in the absolute sense'* or *'life as God has it'*. God's intent for the world was for it to be exactly the way God has it; for it to reflect the culture of Heaven, not for it to

29

be a place of empty chaos and confusion.

BACK TO THE DELIGHTFUL PLACE

It is commonly mistaken today that the Garden that God placed Adam and Eve in was Eden, but the Bible specifically tells us in Genesis 2:8 that it was *"eastward IN Eden,"* denoting that Eden wasn't actually a garden, but a much larger region that contained or housed "a garden". The name Eden itself means *"delightful spot"*, *"presence of God"* or *"Paradise"*. After God created Adam, He wanted to place him in an environment that reflected the culture of Heaven.

Genesis 2:10-14 says:

"[10]Now a river went out of Eden to water the garden, and from there it parted and became four riverheads. [11] The name of the first is Pishon; it is the one which skirts the whole land of Havilah, where there is gold. [12] And the gold

of that land is good. Bdellium and the onyx stone are there. ¹³ *The name of the second river is Gihon; it is the one which goes around the whole land of Cush.* ¹⁴ *The name of the third river is Hiddekel; it is the one which goes toward the east of Assyria. The fourth river is the Euphrates."*

So let's read the scripture in its context. The Bible tells us that a river flowed *"out of"* Eden and then does something that most rivers don't. It splits into four heads, or four other rivers that flowed into this same garden that was inside of Eden.

- The first river *Pishon*, in Hebrew means 'to jump' or 'to bounce' and refers to the strong stream of the water. In this river there is gold (which is good) and also, bdellium and onyx there and the Pishon represented bounty, rich, beauty and life-giving water that never ran dry.

- The second river, *Ghion*, in Hebrew means "bursting forth". This river was larger and very thriving!
- The third river, *Hiddkel*, "*is the one that goes towards the east of Assyria*". It was rapid constant and always flowing.
- And the fourth river, *Euphrates*, means fruitfulness and is also the longest river today! Of these four, Euphrates is the only river that can be found by archeologists today.

The symbolisms of these four rivers all represent characteristics of Heaven. Once the river went out of Eden to water the garden, it began to be filled with the bounty, the beauty, the riches, and the fruitfulness of Heaven! We see in Genesis 2:15 that after the garden was watered by the dew of Heaven, it was then that it was called this delightful place, or what many Christians know today as, "*the Garden of Eden*".

But the garden isn't what made Eden.

Eden is what made the garden. Before the garden was watered it was just like any regular garden that had trees, flowers and plants but no glory. Once it was watered with the dew of Heaven it became the Garden *of Eden* (the delightful place, God's Garden, Paradise or Heaven on earth). This is why no archeologist today can find the Garden of Eden, because it wasn't an actual place, it was the atmosphere of Heaven.

After the garden was watered, God put Adam inside to tend and to keep (Genesis 2:15). God placed Adam in the garden for two reasons: (1) to make sure that nothing defiled or unholy entered in and (2) to see what man would do inside of His presence. God's intent was to bring heaven to earth and for a moment...Eden was our heaven on earth.

Now just imagine Eden, a place of pure bliss. I mean, Adam and Eve were really living the life that we all fantasize of living today! Eden was an environment where no sickness, disease, pain or death existed. There were never any natural disasters and it never rained because God caused a mist to go up from the earth that watered the whole face of the ground. (Genesis 2:4 NKJV) Eden was an environment where no one experienced any form of calamity. It was a place where the weather pattern was never their concern because it never fluctuated. It was always perfect, never too hot or too cold, but always just right.

In Eden, there was never a lack of or a need of anything because everything and anything that Adam and Eve could ever want and need was found in God. He was their source, their supplier and sustainer. Adam and Eve never went hunger or thirsty because Genesis 2:9 says, *"And out of the ground the Lord God made every tree grow that is pleasant to the sight and good for food..."* God supplied them with food that would have lasted them for all of eternity.

But most importantly, Eden was an environment where Adam and Eve enjoyed in constant communion and fellowship with the Lord. Eden was definitely a place where man got to experience the immaculacy of God's creation.

Have you ever daydreamed or even imagined of a perfect place such as this? A place filled with so much delight and bliss? A place where we didn't really have to try and supplicate the presence of God because we actually lived there? I think we all have at one point in our lives. With thoughts such as: *"If only everyone would love each other then we wouldn't have any hatred or violence in this world"* and *"If everyone genuinely cared for each other then no one would ever lack anything and poverty wouldn't exist."* usually plaguing our minds, I believe that God causes us to have these imaginations so that we can see how He originally intended life to be like for all of creation. When we daydream about living in such a perfect place; a place of no suffering, no pain, no sickness, no disease, we are subconsciously longing for this to become our reality again.

We are so limited in our understanding and our finite minds cannot fully grasp it but

God causes our imaginations to bear witness that such a place did, and in fact, does exist!

But how can this be? How can such a perfect place exist? Our minds are so caught up with the state of the world today and it is just absolutely impossible for us to believe that such a perfect place actually existed. It seems so improbable, so unrealistic and just too dag on good to be true. Well, once upon a time, life was "good" and it was "true." This is not some fairytale or a figment of your imagination. There was a time where Heaven was on earth and oh how creation longs to bring it back!

Before all of the destruction, before the hatred and the chaos that we see today, an Eden existed. A world without sin existed and its occurrence took place in the beginning (before Genesis Chapter 3). It was just God and His creation. Remember what God said after He finished creating creation? He said that it was *"very good"*. Oh how creation longs for its Creator to hear Him say those very words again! Oh how desperately creation longs to go back to the beginning! Back to where everything was perfect, back to where it can live up to the full measure and extent of what God has created it for—which was to give glory to God.

ALL OF CREATION AWAITS

Creation has been waiting for this for a very long time. It has been moaning and groaning and labors with birth pangs up until now. It has been waiting for an awakening in the body of Christ, a calling forth of God's Sons in the earth. It has been waiting for the Sons of God to take their rightful stance in the earth! Creation can't go back to the beginning without you; it can't fulfill its purpose without you! Why? Because you were the only one that was there at the beginning after God created all of creation! You are the only one that God has endowed with dominion, with power and with authority in the earth.

2,000 years ago Jesus Christ came to earth and paid the price for all of mankind's sins. The curse of sin was broken and salvation and freedom was freely offered to us all. You have already received your salvation and your freedom but now creation is saying, *"What about me?! When will I be free?!"*

Salvation is for all men, but freedom is for all of creation. Creation knows who you are. It knows how powerful you are. It knows that you hold the key to their freedom. It recognizes you and has been waiting for you! But the problem is, you don't know yourself. You don't know who you are. You don't know how powerful you are. You don't know how important you are. You don't know even know who your Father in Heaven is.

And so, the question lies, when will creation be restored back to its original intent and be freed from its curse?

As soon as you figure out who you are.

2

THE FALL OF ALL OF CREATION

Romans 8:20 "Against its will, all of creation was subject

to God's curse..." (NIV)

Many times when we allude to the word "creation" we think of nature which, by definition, is all of the animals and plants in the world and all the features, forces, and processes that exist or happen independently of people, such as the weather, the sea, mountains, reproduction, and growth. When we categorize creation as solely being nature then we fail to include ourselves as being a part of God's divine creation.

The Fall of Man triggered this selfish response out of us and caused us to conclude that nature (or "creation") is dead and has no direct association with us. This is why we can liter today and not care about the harmful effects that it causes the earth. This is why we see a lot of oil spills happening around us. This is why animals are dying all around the world and we could care less. And this is why global warming has been a huge societal issue that has been around for literally thousands of years. Interestingly enough, human beings are the cause of all of nature's negative effects but for some reason we still seem to act like we have no association with it.

WORKING TOGETHER

But Romans 8:28 says, *"And we know that God causes everything to work together for the good of those who love God and are called according to his purpose for them."* This Scripture clearly states that God causes all things to work together for two associations.

The first is for *those who love Him.*

Human beings are the only species on earth that are capable of loving so that automatically refers to us. And the second association is for *those who are called according to His purpose*. Now here's a huge shocker, humans are not the only created things who have been purposed by God. Everything that God created has a purpose and yes, this includes the trees, the sun, the plants, the animals, the different seasons and even the different weather patterns. But in some vast and infinite way, God makes it all work together for all of creation's good! Although, everything that God created each has its own unique purpose, at the end of the day, all of those unique purposes point back to one specific purpose and that is to glorify Him!

The purpose that God has called all of creation to was (and still is) to glorify Him!

Let's take a look at one of the many ways in which God makes all things work together for all of creation.

Take the sun for example. The sun is a living and breathing organism. God's purpose behind creating the sun has multiple reasons. In regards to man, God created the sun to give us light, heat and energy in order to sustain us while on earth. The sun makes it so easy for us to live because it fosters a comfortable and warm atmosphere for us to live in. We use the sun for more things than we know. We use it to plant vegetation, as a source of vitamin D for our skin, and to pursue the causality things that we enjoy like going to the beach in the summer, taking a hike or just going out for a run. We would never be able to do any of these things if the sun wasn't able to provide us the light and heat that we need. The light that the sun serves a huge purpose in this world. It brings so much beauty to this earth and without it there would be no life at all.

In regards to plants; plants use the sun's energy for photosynthesis, which is the process they use to make food. They store the food in their leaves and the energy flows to other animals that eat the leaves. When leaves fall, decomposers (which are in the soil) work on it, with the help of moisture and heat from the sun.

A plant will capture the sun's light rays in a chloroplast through a chemical reaction and this conversion gives plants the ability to supply calories to all life. It is through plants that cows are fed and through cows that humans are fed. In this way, sunlight provides the source of food for all of life on earth! How amazing is that?!

In regards to animals; Sunlight is vital for all animals, even though different animals need different amounts of sunlight. Animals need the sun so that the plants can produce food for them to eat.

All in all, both animals and humans depend on plants and plants depend on the sun. There is a cycle of dependency going on between all of creation and the moment one feature or force stops working then the dependent are left with no other choice than to figure out another source of living or they will eventually die. If the sun stops fulfilling its purpose, or falls short of the glory of which God created it for (which is to give off light and energy) then the animals, plants and humans all lose their dependency and will eventually die.

THE DECLARATION OF INDEPENDENCE

The moment Adam sinned; he declared independence from God and lost his identity, purpose, dependency on God and his rights as a Son. The moment Adam bit the apple is the moment he decided to fall short of God's original intent for His life, which was to be a Kingdom representative of Heaven on earth and to dominate the earth with the culture of Heaven. Adam's act of treason caused him to lose contact with his original country. That's why Romans 5:12 says, *"When Adam sinned, sin entered the world. Adam's sin brought death, so death spread to everyone, for everyone sinned."* So when Adam sinned, not only did all of mankind sin but all of creation sinned because Adam was the one that gave name to all the wild animals and the birds of the air. He was the one who God entrusted to tend and watch over the garden. He was the one that God placed in charge of everything that was in the garden but he blew it! That's why God said to Adam, in Genesis 3:12 *"...the ground is cursed because of you."*

Through Adam's one sin, his dependency on God was cut off and it meant that he no longer needed God. So he adapted a new way of living; a life of death that entailed complete separation from God, who is the Giver of Life Himself.

OH, AMERICA!

When a country declares independence from a colony they develop a new lifestyle and culture. This lifestyle would entail new morals, new behaviors, new mannerisms and new laws. Before the United States of America became an independent nation, they were under the governmental influence of Great Britain. The American colonists were completely influenced by the culture of Great Britain and adapted their way of doing life. The Americans took on everything that the British did, from their dialect, to what they eat, how they dressed, to their habits and morals. The American colonists were also fully dependent on Great Britain for everything.

But something happened. The American Colonists thought that they were being treated unfairly by the British because they were making them pay unreasonable taxes on tea and postage stamps. There was nothing they could do to stop this because they had neither rights nor representation of themselves in the British Parliament. The British and the American Colonists went back and forth with each other for what seemed like years at a time.

As time went on, tensions continued rising between both colonies that resulted in violence and wars. So on July 4th, 1776 the American Colonists called it quits. Congress signed The Declaration of Independence which declared that the 13 colonies (which are now a part of the 50 United States) were free from British rule and all political affiliations with Great Britain. The United States now became a free country with no governing allies or rulers.

Over 200 years and over 40 presidents

later, The United States of America is still an independent country. America now has her own territories, her own culture, her own citizens, her own government and her own democracy. Sure enough, America got what she wanted. She wanted ruler-ship, she wanted power, she wanted sov14ginity and she wanted to govern.

America has passed laws and made many rulings that *"seemed right"* based on democracy but in the end, they will eventually lead to death. Proverbs 14: 12 says, *"There is a way that seems right to a man, but its end is the way to death."* The apple *seemed* right; it *seemed* pleasing, it *seemed* alluring, it *seemed* convincing and the serpent made disobeying God *"seem right"* by lying to Adam and Eve and saying *""You won't die!"* in Genesis 3:4. But after they ate the apple, Genesis 3:23 says, *"So the Lord God banished them from the Garden of Eden..."* So we see that this way that *"seemed right"* to Adam and Eve resulted in death. It resulted in separation from Eden, the very presence of God.

America was once a nation that was

founded on biblical principles and Christian morals and character. It was a nation that was once under God and once upon a time it lived up to the allegiance that we so boldly and confidently pledge. It was once a nation that was under God, indivisible, with liberty and justice for all. But just like Adam, America too declared independence from God. America wanted her own way of living; she wanted her own morals, her own customs, her own beliefs, and her own system. America wanted democracy when God intended for a Kingdom.

And in response to this, here is what God did in Romans 1:24-32:

"So God abandoned them to do whatever shameful things their hearts desired. As a result, they did vile and degrading things with each other's bodies. [25] They traded the truth about God for a lie. So they worshiped and served the things God created instead of the Creator himself, who is worthy of eternal praise! Amen. [26] That is why God abandoned them to their shameful desires. Even the women turned against the natural way to have sex and

instead indulged in sex with each other. [27] And the men, instead of having normal sexual relations with women, burned with lust for each other. Men did shameful things with other men, and as a result of this sin, they suffered within themselves the penalty they deserved. [28] Since they thought it foolish to acknowledge God, he abandoned them to their foolish thinking and let them do things that should never be done. [29] Their lives became full of every kind of wickedness, sin, greed, hate, envy, murder, quarreling, deception, malicious behavior, and gossip. [30] They are backstabbers, haters of God, insolent, proud, and boastful. They invent new ways of sinning, and they disobey their parents. [31] They refuse to understand, break their promises, are heartless, and have no mercy. [32] They know God's justice requires that those who do these things deserve to die, yet they do them anyway. Worse yet, they encourage others to do them, too."

Since America thought it foolish to stop acknowledging God in the economy, in the school systems, in politics, in media, in entertainment, in the government and in everything else, God abandoned America to herself to do whatever shameful thing her heart desired to do. And now the underlying question is "Why?"; "Why did God abandon America to herself?", "Why did God let Adam and Eve eat the apple?", "Why didn't He just come down and intervene and cause everything to be perfect?"

GOD'S INTENT FOR A KINGDOM

Man is so impatient; we are always so quick to try and figure out the why of things without first understanding the intent. When it comes to the things of God or anything in life, the question of "Why?" will always lead you in a dubious place until you understand what I like to call, God's NIR. Or in other words, God's nature, intent and reasoning. If you don't understand God's nature, intent and reasoning then you will always question everything in life.

To understand why God abandoned America to herself, to understand why God didn't stop Adam and Eve from sinning, to understand why there are is so much chaos in the world; you must first understand God's intent behind creating the world. Once you understand His nature, then you will understand His intentions. And once you understand His intentions, then you will understand His reasoning. God is a good a good God. He is an almighty, all-wise and all-knowing and only desires for His people the very best. Because His nature only allows Him to desire for His people the best, He wouldn't have it any other way than to intend for all of creation to be a Kingdom. Yes, God's intent for creation was Kingdom. God's intent for America was a Kingdom. He had a plan before the foundations of the world that involved the Kingdom of Heaven invading earth. His reason was because He wanted to create a place that looked like the original home (Heaven).

There are so man-made ideologies, theologies and philosophies that have been created with the intent of making the world a better place. From imperialism, to colonialism, to socialism, to communism and now to "our best one yet", democracy! Man has continued to come up with many –ism's with the intent of making this world a better place. But none of these can ever work, even with our most recent and popular one (democracy). It can never work because God's original plan was to establish a Kingdom! The Kingdom can never be replaced nor can it ever be seen as an alternative because the Kingdom is it!

God's intent was to establish the Kingdom of Heaven on earth and to dominate the earth with His Sons. But because God is a righteous and sovereign God He has given Himself no jurisdiction on earth. God gave man the power to rule and dominate the earth exactly how it is in Heaven. That's why the Psalmist said, *"The highest heavens belong to the LORD, but the earth he has given to mankind."* (Psalm 115:16) But God also gave man free will, He gave America the free will to choose and she chose democracy instead of a

Kingdom.

Everything you see today in the world is a result of one thing—sin. The issue is not that our justice system is twisted; it's not that our police are corrupt people; it's not that our political leaders are ignorant (although these may be causes of it). The preliminary issue is, *"For all have sinned and fallen short of God's glorious standard." (Romans 3:23)* Because of Adam's sin, everything in all of creation fell short of God's glorious standard and purpose for this world. What is this standard? The standard is holiness! The standard is righteousness! The standard is purity! And the purpose was to establish the Kingdom of Heaven here on earth!

All of creation has fallen short of God's glorious standard and now we are killing each other, bombing up different nations, professing to different man-made religions and just full blown losing our minds trying to get back to this standard that was once ours! We are all trying to get back to get back to Eden, back to our delightful place... back to the Kingdom!

THE SEARCH FOR KINGDOM

None of us are different. We are all the same. Buried deep inside the heart of every man is a search, a desperate longing for an ideal world. We all desire an Eden—a place of no destruction, no chaos, no pain, no sickness, no disease, no gossip, and no hatred. Deep down inside we all want the same thing and if you ask 200 different people what they want to do in life, you will come to find out that those same 200 people all have one thing in common, and that is that their destiny, their purpose, the reason why they exist in this life is all tied to making this world a better place.

All of our visions, talents, aspirations, and goals are all tied and connected to bettering this world. Whether it's becoming a doctor, a motivational speaker, a governor, or even the next President of the United States; all of these professions tie to one thing and that is making the world a better place. Imagine if the entire human race came together and realized that we all want the same thing? Killings will stop. Murders will stop. Fighting, envy, jealousy, covetousness and malice will all stop once we realize that we are all in search for the same thing and that we, subconsciously, are all in this together.

Dr. Martin Luther King once said, "*We must all learn to live together as brothers or we will all perish together as fools. We are tied together in the single garment of destiny, caught in an inescapable network of mutuality. And whatever affects one directly affects all indirectly. For some strange reason I can never be what I ought to be until you are what you ought to be. This is the way God's universe is made; this is the way it is structured.*"

If we learn to realize that we are all in this together, then racism will cease to exist, then discrimination and competition and hatred will dissipate. No wonder why Psalm 133:11 says, *"Behold, how good and how pleasant it is for brothers to dwell together in unity!"*

That man didn't really want to blow up

the elementary school; the police officer really didn't want to shoot the black male, the 21 year-old girl didn't really want to commit suicide. We are all just tired and frustrated of living in such a corrupt world and our hearts are desperately aching for the Kingdom again. We all just want to get back to this place that was once ours. We are all in search for the same thing but just using different routes, doing different things and testing out different religions trying to get there.

Everything we do in this life is because we are searching for this ideal place. This search implies that we lost something that was once ours, and indeed we did. You cannot search for what you never had so this means that deep down inside we all know that a perfect world existed but we just lost it. We lost the Kingdom. We lost our identity. We lost our purpose and what we see in our world today is millions of people who are spending their entire lives searching for the Kingdom through drugs, sex, mediums, witchcraft, religions, relationships and so many other things.

GOOD NEWS: THE KINGDOM IS IT!

But there is good news to be told! Once you find the Kingdom, you can stop searching because everything that you have been searching for is found in the Kingdom of God! Matthew 13:45-46 says, *"Again, the kingdom of heaven is like a merchant in search of fine pearls. When he found one very precious pearl, he went away and sold all he had and bought it."* Nothing can replace the Kingdom. The Kingdom is it. The Kingdom is the pearl. It's the thing that you have been searching for all along!

Isaiah 6:7-9 says, *"For a child is born to us, a son is given to us. The government will rest on his shoulders. And he will be called: Wonderful Counselor, Mighty God, Everlasting Father, Prince of Peace. His government and its peace will never end. He will rule with fairness and justice from the throne of his ancestor David for all eternity. The passionate commitment of the LORD of Heaven's Armies will make this happen!"*

After sin entered into the world through Adam, we lost everything that was ours (which was the Kingdom). But when Jesus Christ came to earth, He came to bring the Kingdom of Heaven back to earth! It's God's way of saying, "Okay let's try to this again but this time around, I'm going to send my Son and He's going to show everyone how it's really supposed to be done."

If you read throughout the four Gospels, you will find that everywhere that Jesus went, He didn't preach religion, He didn't preach doctrine and He didn't preach about a democracy; He preached the message of the Kingdom!

- In Matthew 4:7, He told us to *"Repent, for the **kingdom of heaven** is near!"*
- In John 3:3, He tells us the only way to see the Kingdom is through salvation! *"Jesus declared, "I tell you the truth; no one can see the*

kingdom of God *unless he is born again."*

- In Matthew 6:33, He told us to make the Kingdom our number one priority. *"**But seek first his kingdom** and his righteousness, and all these things will be given to you as well."*

- In Matthew 6:10 He told us to pray for the Kingdom to come to earth just like it is in Heaven. *"Pray then like this: "Our Father in heaven, hallowed be your name. **Your kingdom come**, your will be done, on earth as it is in heaven."*

- He told us in Luke 12:32 that God was pleased to give us the Kingdom. *"Do not be afraid, little flock, for your Father has been pleased to give you the **kingdom**."*

- In Matthew 16: 19 He gave us the keys to the Kingdom! *"And I will give **you the keys of the Kingdom of Heaven**, Whatever you forbid on earth will be forbidden in* *heaven, and whatever you permit on earth will be permitted in heaven."*

- John 18:36 Jesus said, *"**My kingdom** is not of this world. If it were, my servants would fight to prevent my arrest by the Jews. But now my kingdom is from another place."*

- In Matthew 18:3-4, He tells us who the greatest are in the Kingdom. *"Then he said, "I tell you the truth, unless you turn from your sins and become like little children, you will never get into the **Kingdom of Heaven**. So anyone who becomes as humble as this little child is the greatest in the **Kingdom of Heaven**."*

- In Luke 7:20-21, He tells us that the Kingdom of God actually lives inside of us. (*"Once, having been asked by the Pharisees when **the kingdom of God** would come, Jesus replied, "**The kingdom of**</*

*God does not come with your careful observation, nor will people say, 'Here it is,' or 'There it is,' because **the kingdom of God is within you.**")*

These are just a few of many Scriptures that Jesus spoke about pertaining to the Kingdom of Heaven. So you see, Jesus Christ came to give us back our inheritance to the Kingdom and our rights as Sons of God. He came to give us back that which we lost! The search is now over! We no longer have to search for the Kingdom in anything ever again! After Genesis 3, we lost our culture but Jesus came to restore it back to us. This is why we must repent, receive salvation, get filled with the Holy Spirit and read and study the Scriptures to get back in touch with our culture (the Kingdom of Heaven) and our identity as Sons.

To live out the original intent and purpose for our lives, we are to live it from a Kingdom perspective; a heavenly perspective.

In Colossians 3: 2 Paul tells us to, *"Think about the things of heaven, not the things of the earth."* As Sons of God we must be continually trained in godliness and think about the things above. Why? Because as a man thinks in his heart so is he. If we constantly think about the realities of Heaven, then those things will begin to manifest it in our day to day lives and eventually seep out into the world that we live in.

We constantly hear quotes such as, "the change we want to see must first begins in me", well it's true. The moment we begin to re-familiarize and reconnect ourselves back to the Kingdom of God, change will immediately sweep in and invade every area our lives and we will be compelled to pray prayers like Jesus instructs us to in Matthew 6:10 *("May your Kingdom come soon. May your will be done on earth, as it is in heaven.")* and see the world around us change!

Once we get this message about the Kingdom, our job is to go out and preach it to all of creation! Once you have found what you've been looking for, now it's time to get out of the church and preach it to the homeless, the destitute, the forgotten and the prostitutes! Preach the message that the Kingdom that we once lost, has now been found! This is the key to setting creation free from its curse! It's preaching the Kingdom!

Romans 8:20 says, *"Against its will, all of creation was subjected to God's curse. But with eager hope, the creation looks forward to the day when it will join God's children in glorious free from death and decay."* All of creation has been looking forward to the day when the Sons of God would get the revelation about the Kingdom of God and the role we play in the Kingdom because once we do, creation knows that they will join us in glorious freedom!

The Kingdom is it! Mark 16:15 *"And He said to them, "Go into all the world and preach the gospel to every creature."*

IT'S UP TO THE SONS

If we as Sons of God do our jobs correctly, the earth should look like Heaven. The reality of Heaven will soon become our reality here on earth. Once we find what we've been looking for then it is our job to go out and tell people to stop looking because the Kingdom is neither here nor there. It's not in Hollywood, it's not in the political government, it's not in weed, it's not in that fraternity or sorority, it's not in parties but the Kingdom of God is within.

We cannot continue to use the events that are going on in the world as an excuse to idly sit by and do nothing when God has given us complete jurisdiction and reign over the earth. In Matthew 24:14 Jesus says, *"And this gospel of the kingdom will be preached in the whole world as a testimony to all nations, and then the end will come."* What does this mean? If we continue putting the Kingdom in the future, we will never experience it now. *"On earth...as it is in Heaven."* Heaven can become our reality now! We can experience love, joy, peace, justice and see an end to sickness and poverty now! Jesus did not die so that we can idly sit by and wait for Him to return. No! Jesus died so that we can experience the fullness of all that He has called us to here on earth exactly how it is in Heaven!

Genesis 1:1 says, *"In the beginning God created the heavens and the earth."* The earth was never created to function without Heaven. The heavens were created before the earth because earth was created to be a colony of Heaven. The Bible only makes mention of the earth being formless, dark and empty. It never mentioned the same for Heaven because Heaven was already created. God wanted to fill the earth with everything that Heaven already inhabited. So He created light, vegetation, trees, fruit and animals on earth because He wanted earth to reflect the Kingdom of Heaven. The only thing that Heaven didn't have was man. So God created man to administrate the Kingdom of Heaven on earth. Heaven has a ruler and that is God. But the earth, He gave to man to dominate. He gave us everything we needed to rule, to govern, to protect, to steward and to authorize the earth so everything that we see happening in our world today is not God's fault, it's ours.

We have been pointing the finger at God and blaming Him for all of our mess for entirely too long but now is time for us to mature and own up to our responsibilities here on earth.

We are responsible for this earth. At the end our lives, God is going to ask us what we did with the earth. Did we just abandon it to the enemy? Did we just wait for His return? Or did we do what He has called and created us to do? Did we do what He has commanded of us and preached the Good News of the Kingdom of God to all of creation?

Many believers do not understand the message of the Kingdom of God and this is what is causing so much confusion within the body of Christ. We don't even know what to do with all that's going on in this world, so our response is to just continue attending regular Sunday service and hope that our church attendance will bring about change. Oh and let's not forget to actually post 2nd Chronicles 4:17 on all of our social media accounts twice a daily.

Because of our lack of ignorance and understanding about the message of the Kingdom, we go around "prophesying" that the end of the world is coming and that Jesus Christ is coming back but what we fail to realize is that we are the ones that actually hold the return of Jesus in our hands. Scripture says that no man knows the hour or day of His return, but it is surely contingent on the message of the Kingdom of God being preached.

The Bible says that He has given us the keys to the Kingdom. As Sons of God, we are not here to bring people to Heaven, that's God's job. The only way that a man can enter Heaven is through Jesus. Our job is to unlock the door of the Kingdom and bring the Kingdom of Heaven to earth! Once we start doing our job right, all of creation will stop groaning.

REVEALING OF THE SONS OF GOD

.

3

SONSHIP IS THE IDENTIFER

*"The Spirit you received does not make you slaves,
so that you live in fear again; rather, the Spirit you
received brought about your adoption to sonship. And by
him we cry, "Abba, Father."*
Romans 8:15 (NIV)

According to Webster's Dictionary, "Identity" is defined as: the name of a person; or the qualities and beliefs that make a particular person or group different from others. But identity is not just who a person is; it's not just the different qualities or traits that a person inhabits. Identity is not what or who a person believes in. It's not what you think, what you've accomplished or what your gifts and talents are. Yes, all of these different characteristics can help attribute to one's own identity but the truth of the matter is that all of these things are meaningless if you have yet to receive love of God the Father.

Receiving the love that God has for you is the foundation of knowing who you are. You were created and fashioned by love Himself and the only way that you can come to know who you truly are is by revisiting this love.

1ˢᵗ John 4:9 says, *"God showed how much he loved us by sending his one and only Son into the world so that we might have eternal life through him. This is real love-not that we loved God, but that he loved us and sent his Son as a sacrifice to take away our sins."* God didn't just send Jesus into the world to save you from your sins. He sent him to restore your identity back to you and the only way He could have done this is through love.

This same love was designed to bring you to a full revelation of who you truly are as a Son of God. All of you have to do is receive this love through joining in an intimate relationship with the Father. It is not until you respond to Him and allow this love to be perfected in you that you will begin to walk in the truest form of who you were created to be.

Ephesians 1:4 says, "*…just as He chose us in Him before the foundation of the world, that we should be holy and without blame before Him in love, having predestined us to adoption as sons by Jesus Christ Himself, according to the good pleasure of His will.*" In love, your identity as a Son was placed inside of you way before God even put you in your mother's womb. But when sin entered into the world, your true identity became trapped and hidden and can now only be found and revealed to you through restoration and reconciliation with the Father.

1st John 3:1 says, *"Behold, what manner of love the Father hath bestowed upon us, that we should be called the children (sons) of God."* You were created by God and purposed by God in love and until you realize that the motivation behind your existence was simply the love that the Father has for you, then Sonship will be always be unattainable. Coming to the full knowledge and full revelation of the truest form of who you are as a Son will always be so hard for you to acquire because no matter how hard you try to attribute your identity to how well you play the bass, or how well you sing or how well dress, it will never measure up to knowing that you are greatly loved by the Creator of the Universe.

It will seem like you're trying to solve the mystery of who you are because it may "seem" like God is hiding it from you, but God is such a good Father and deeply desires for you to come to the full revelation of who you are as a Son.

When we don't receive the love of the Father, we, in turn are rejecting the very essence of who we are. Think of it this way. You are everything that God says you are. And according to His Word (which by the way, cannot be nullified) He says that you are loved, that you are cherished, and that you are the apple of His eye. But when you fail to accept these truths, you not only reject Him, you reject your identity and you make Him out to be a liar.

God is so into you and He loved you so much that He sent His only Son into this world to die a brutal and gruesome death. And He did this all for your sake. The only way you can come to know your truest identity is through having a relationship with the Father and this can only be formed through accepting Jesus Christ into your life. (This may sound redundant, but I promise, it is no typo, I just want to emphasis the importance of having this relationship). If you prayed the prayer back in Chapter 1, then congratulations again because the decision that you made just propelled you into walking in your identity as a Son!

Salvation is more than just you being saved from hell; it's also a restoration of your identity! In John 14:16, Jesus says, *"I am the way and the truth and the life. No one comes to the Father except through me."* Jesus is the way. There is no other way to get around it. Your identity doesn't come from nor can it be found in anything else. Not in your degree, your job, your relationship status or even by how much money you own. Your identity can only be found in Jesus!

JESUS INTRODUCES SONSHIP

Sonship is a relational level of intimacy and maturity that Christ had with God the Father while on earth and it's the level that He desires for all of His children to get to.

If you read through the four Gospels you see how Jesus knew His Father. Like really *knew* Him. The level of intimacy and maturity that Jesus had in His relationship with God was on a completely different level compared to that of the disciples.

There were times that Jesus would tell the disciples something and they wouldn't understand because they were not yet mature. For example in Luke 18: 31-34 Jesus was telling his disciples about how the prophecies of his death told by the prophets were going to be fulfilled but verse 34 says *"But they (the disciples) didn't understand any of this. The significance of his words was hidden from them, and they failed to grasp what he was talking about."* They didn't understand because they weren't mature and had yet to reach a level of intimacy with God the Father.

The cross was not only an expression of God's love for the world, but a very important process by which Sonship would be revealed to all of mankind. Jesus came to reveal to us our true identity as Sons of God by first, manifesting Himself on earth as The Firstborn Son.

When Jesus came to earth, He forsook His identity as The Firstborn Son. Does this mean that He wasn't God while on earth? Absolutely not! Jesus was still fully God but also fully man. But He spent practically all of his life on earth having to re-learn Sonship all for our sake. Jesus wanted to show us how a man on earth, who fully understood His identity as Son was supposed to live. He wanted to show us how we should walk, talk and operate in complete power, authority and dominion as a Son by allowing this all to flow from a having a genuine relationship with the Father.

There is nothing doctrinal, religious, superstitious, or structured about Sonship. The only protocol to Sonship is relationship. It is only through a place of intimacy with the Father that Sonship is revealed, restored and manifested. Sonship is ultimately why Jesus came and it was God's original idea for His kids from the very beginning. Although sin hid it, it can never nullify God's original plan! Your identity as a Son must be revealed. It has to.

Hebrews 2:10 says, *"God, for whom and through whom everything was made, chose to bring many children [sons] into glory. And it was only right that he should make Jesus, through his suffering, a perfect leader, fit to bring them into their salvation."* (NLT) Through this scripture we see that God chose to bring us into glory (into Sonship) and he chose Jesus, The Firstborn Son, to be our leader, our pioneer, our captain, to lead us into

Sonship which comes first by receiving salvation.

The only way that Jesus could effectively express the truest form of His identity as a Son was to position Himself to be with the Father. That's why in many instances in the Bible, you see that Jesus often *"withdrew to lonely places to pray"* (Luke 5:16) and never lived His life without abiding with the Father. From a place of abiding with God, Jesus was able to only do as the Father does, to say what the Father says and to only act as the Father acts. Everything that Jesus did flowed from that familial relationship with His Father.

Here are some scriptural references that show how much Jesus valued the intimacy that he shared with His Father.

- **John 5:19** *"So I tell you the truth, the Son can do nothing by himself. He does only what he sees the Father doing. Whatever the Father does, the Son also does."*

- **John 12:49-50** *"I don't speak on my own authority. The Father who sent me has commanded what to say and how to say it. And I know his commands lead to eternal life; so I say whatever the Father tells me to say."*
- **John 10:30** *""I and the Father are one."*
- **John 14:31** **"...**but so that the world may know that I love the Father, I do exactly as the Father commanded Me."*

The only way that Jesus was able to speak about the Father in such an intimate way was through relationship. It was through being in constant fellowship and communion with Him because Jesus understood that a part of the Father, He could do *no*-thing.

Apart from the Father, He couldn't effectively go out to speak for the Father with such boldness. Apart from the Father, Jesus wouldn't have been able to effectively operate in signs, wonders, and miracles. Apart from the Father, Jesus wouldn't have been able to show compassion, love and mercy to those who constantly persecuted Him. Apart from the Father, He wouldn't even have been able to go to the cross and bear the weight of sin of all of humanity on His back. Jesus understood that He could not do anything apart from the Father and He made it his number one priority to dwell in the secret place of the Most High and abide under the shadow of the   Almighty.

CONFIDENCE THAT COMES WITH BEING A SON

Jesus Christ has so many different names and was called these many different names by people all throughout the Bible. And even today we still call Him the Messiah, the King of Kings, the Lord of Lords, Rabbi, some say He is a Prophet, but we know Him a our Healer, Provider, Protector, Deliver. He's also known as The Bright and Morning Star,

Jehovah, Yeshua and the list goes on and on and on. But the one name that Jesus identified Himself with the most was *'Son of God'*. Out of all the things that He was called in Scripture, He referred to Himself as not even the Savior of the World, but as a Son.

We see this when He was asked before the council of men in Luke 22:70, *"Are you the Son of God?"* and Jesus responds by saying, *"You rightly say that I am."* The confidence that was portrayed in His response came from knowing who His Father was. This confidence and boldness exuded not only His speech, but in His posture, His conduct and in His character. His confidence did not come from who He was, but *of* whom He was and He was *of* God.

After Jesus was baptized in the Jordan River by His cousin John, He was led into the wilderness by the Spirit of God and the first thing that the devil tempted Him with was questioning His identity as a Son. Matthew 4:3 says,

"Now when the tempter came to Him, he said, "If You are the Son of God, command that these stones become bread." But because Jesus already had a revelatory knowledge of whom He was as the Son of God, He was able to boldly and confidently shut the devil up and refute him with the Word by saying, *"No! The Scriptures say, Man should not live by bread alone but by every word that comes from the mouth of God."* (Matthew 4:4)

Jesus knew that He was the Son of God, and so did the devil. The devil isn't dumb; he knows how powerful knowing your identity is. This is why identity was the first thing the devil tested Jesus with because he knows that once you get to a place of realizing who you are as a Son of God then no power in hell can stand against you. The devil is terrified of people who know their identities because he knows that cannot be moved or shaken.

We see throughout Scripture how Jesus didn't even have to prove His identity to the devil because His Father already affirmed it in Matthew 3:17 when He said, *"This is my beloved Son, in whom I am well pleased".* The Father wasn't pleased with Jesus because He went into the wilderness; He was pleased with Him because He was His Son. It was the pleasing affirmation that the Father gave Jesus that allowed Him to go into the wilderness to be tempted by the devil. Jesus was actually led into the wilderness by the Spirit of God but it was in that place of testing and discipline that Jesus was able to withstand the devils temptations and stand firm in His identity.

All Jesus did was say what His Father had already said through His Word and that was His defense—the spoken Word of God. In that moment, He was acting in His identity as a Son. Being a Son of God was the name that Jesus most resonated with because He knew that He couldn't be a healer, a teacher, a friend, a brother or even the Savior of the World outside of Sonship. Jesus knew that everything He did had to flow from His relationship with the Father.

The same goes for us, everything that we do in this life must flow from our relationship with the Father. It must flow from out of a place of knowing that you are loved by God. Why? Because this is where your identity, your confidence, your assurance, your security, your purpose and your destiny lies. It's in your Sonship. Your Sonship is your distinction. It's your identifier. It's what separates you from the others. It's the highest calling on earth and that is why it is so important to God that we get to this place.

LET'S GET BACK

Whether you are a pastor, a teacher, a worship leader, a lawyer or a business woman/man, a husband, a wife, a youth leader at your church or even if you prophesy in the name of the Lord— all of this must flow from out of a place Sonship otherwise there will be a disconnect between you and the Father. God speaks about this disconnect in Matthew 7:22 when He says, *"On judgment day, many will say, "Lord! Lord! We prophesied in your name and cast out demons in your name and performed many miracles in your name. But I will reply, 'I never knew you. Get away from me, you who break God's laws."*

In this scripture, God is talking about the believers who perform signs and wonders and do all these incredible things for the Kingdom of God without allowing the intimacy of the Father's spirit to align with their spirit. It is very possible for one to operate through the Holy Spirit and move in signs and wonders without knowing their identity as a Son. But without knowing who you are as God's Son, you will never have a true connection with your Father.

The Holy Spirit is the power source behind all the signs and wonders but the Spirit of the Father is the power that raises your identity from the dead and restores to you your identity as a Son so that you can cry out *"Abba! Father!"* God trusts us with His Spirit; if He didn't then He wouldn't have left Him with us here on earth. More than you moving and operating in miracles, signs and wonders through the unction of the Holy Spirit, the Father wants you to know your value, to know your worth, to know your identity. He wants you to know that He is your Daddy and that you are His Son.

There are many different pastors, ministers and worship leaders who we don't hear about anymore because they have fallen into sin and are tied down by the weight of guilt and shame. It's not because they heard God wrong and they weren't actually called to be a pastor, or called to minister or to lead worship, it's because their assigned calling didn't flow from out of a place of Sonship. It's because they didn't have a revelation of who they are as a Son. If they did, then they would know and understand that *"love covers a multitude of sins" (1st Peter 4:8)* and be convinced just as Paul was that *"nothing can ever separate us from God's love (Romans 8:38).* This is the confidence and assurance that comes with being a Son of God. That no matter what you do, who you do it with, or how many times you've done it; one thing's for sure that will forever remain true is that God loves you. This same agape love was designed to awaken your spirit and bring you to the full revelation of who you truly are as a Son of God.

There are also many people who get saved and immediately thrust themselves into ministry out of zealous effort and not because they specifically heard from the Lord out of a place of intimacy. They spend many years in theology school and read the Bible from cover to cover. After theology school, they go back to get their PhD in God the Father, God the Son and God the Holy Spirit. They believe that the more they do for the Kingdom, the more God will love them and this will ultimately be their ticket into Heaven. This is a false and religious mentality to have and this is not how God intended it to be. This is also why many billionaires and famous people don't feel fulfilled. It's because they chase money, they chase, fame, fortune, popularity and reputations but deep down inside they are going through an identity crises, struggling to find out who they really are in this world.

If we fail in looking at the identity aspect first, then we take the focus off of who we are and put the focus on what we are going to accomplish in life or in ministry. Your focus should always be on who you are as a Son and your relationship with your Father, not titles, authority or position.

IT'S TIME

God is tired of partnering with people who aren't walking in Sonship. He's tired of partnering people who have yet to grasp the full revelation of who they are because He's seeing that there is no progression in the body of Christ. Many believers who made the decision to give their lives to the Lord 5, 10 and some even well over 15 years ago are still struggling with the same sin that has been plaguing their lives since before they found Christ. We have been battling with the same sin and dealing with the same heart issues for years and our pastors don't even have the discernment to know because they are too. And we wonder why there is a fracture in the body. We wonder why it seems like the body is immobile. It's because too many of us are hurting. Too many of us are in pain. Too many of us are still harboring unforgiveness in our hearts. Too many of us are still engaging in worldly affairs.

Too many of us are still gossiping, engaging in fornication, and don't even let me touch on the topic of envy that no one likes to talks about. Too many of us secretly desire for ourselves what we see our brothers and sisters have. It's no wonder why this world isn't progressing, it's because the body isn't!

For a long time, there has been no mobility, no growth, no advancement in the body of Christ but God is saying that it's time for us to grow up; it's time for us to mature! We are not babies anymore to continue feeding off of the milk of the Word. We are supposed to be moving from glory to glory but instead we aren't moving at all. He's saying that enough is enough. It's time for the church to arise in power! No more shallow Christianity! No more being wishy-washy with your faith! It's time for us to get ourselves together and deal with every weight of sin that is so easily entangling us. It is time for the body of Christ to mature from children into Sons because all of creation has been waiting for us!

THE DIFFERENCE BETWEEN A CHILD AND A SON

Contrary to popular belief, everyone is not a child of God. This may sound harsh to some of you, but it's the undiluted truth. Yes, we are all apart of God's great creation, and in fact His crowning achievement, but we are not all a part of His royal family. Many people, who have some knowledge of God but haven't accepted His Son into their lives and aren't actively pursuing a lifestyle that reflects Him believe that they are children of God. But how can you claim to be a child of someone that you don't even know? John 1:12 says, *"But to all who believed in Him and accepted Him, He gave the right to become children of God."* The only way one can become a child of God is through accepting the ultimate gift of salvation that was purchased by Jesus Christ. Once you confess with your mouth and believe in your heart that Jesus Christ is the Son of God, you are given rights to become God's child and are accepted into His royal family.

The Greek word for child is *"tekon"*, which means, a young child who is just beginning to learn who they are and who they were created to be and living in complete dependence on their father. When a baby is born, they have to learn basic life skills such as how to walk, how to sit-up on their own, how to run, talk, count and so many other things. But they cannot learn these things on their own; they have to depend on their father (or mother) to supervise them. For example, a child cannot learn how to walk alone because they will end up stumbling and eventually fall.

Once you give your life to Christ, you become awakened to your true self and you now have to re-learn who you are. You have to un-learn some habits and customs that you've adapted in your former life and put on a new way of thinking and learn habits that align with your new way of life.

You are not just a physical being, you are a spiritual being. In fact, you are more spiritual than you are physical but because of sin your spirit is dead. But thank God for the gift of salvation because when you give your life to Jesus Christ, a re-birth happens to you in the spirit that causes your spirit man to become alive again. This is why you usually hear Christians use the terminology "born-again". In John 3:5-6, Jesus says, *"No one can enter the Kingdom of God without being born of water and the Spirit. Humans can only reproduce the human life, but the Holy Spirit gives birth to spiritual life."* (NLT) The moment you made that life changing decision, your spirit man became awakened and now your truest version of self can now be manifested in the earth. But it doesn't happen just like that, in order for your truest self to manifested, it takes time.

Just like with any natural child, you have to learn how to feed yourself, how to clothe yourself, how to tie your shoes, how to use the bathroom on your own, how to write, spell and count. As a child, you must learn all of these things in order to move on to the next stage of your life. This same concept goes for any child of God. We must learn how to feed ourselves with the Word of God daily and not solely depend on The Verse of The Day from the Bible App. We must learn how to crucify our fleshly desires and how to flee from youthful lusts. We must learn how to spend intentional time with the Father and get rid of the jealousy, the gossip, the anger, the bitterness and any other sin that is hindering you from drawing closer to God. Again, all of these things (and many more) are necessary for any child to learn and go through if they are to reach the next level or stage in their lives.

Now, of course as children, God does not expect us to know it all and to perfect everything on the first try. This is why He has graciously given us the Holy Spirit as our Helper —to lead, direct and guide us into the manner and way in which we should go.

But because the church has become stagnant in her growth, God is saying, *"You have been believers so long now that you ought to be teaching others. Instead, you need someone to teach you again the basic things about God's word. You are like babies who need milk and cannot eat solid food."*(Hebrews 5:12)

This scripture refers to children as "babies" and we know that in the natural, babies cannot digest solid food because they have yet to reach the point of growth. Again, it's the same way with us. God cannot entrust children with great works. The Lord cannot reveal to children His plan and purposes for their lives because in 1st Corinthians 3: 2-3, Paul says to the church of Corinth... *"I had to feed you with milk, not with solid food, because you weren't ready for anything stronger. And you still aren't ready, or you are still controlled by your sinful nature. You are jealous of one another and quarrel with each other. Doesn't that prove you are controlled by your sinful nature? Aren't you living like people of the world?"*

The Lord can't entrust His Kingdom and property to children. And we wonder why we are so uncertain when it comes to knowing God's plan and purpose for our lives, or even when it comes to knowing which direction we should take, or even our identity. It's because we have become too comfortable in being just children when the Lord is calling us to a spiritual maturity! God cannot entrust the government of His Kingdom to children. Just like any sane natural father would never ask His child to pay mortgage, or to drive His car, or to pay car note, God the Father will never place anything in your hands that He knows you are not mature enough to handle yet.

Any good natural father does not desire to see any of his children stay in the same place. A good father desires and delights in seeing his child grow, day by day, month by month and year by year and develop into the fullness of his potential as his son. This is the same with our Heavenly Father. He desires to see all of His children mature and grow into the fullness and likeness of who He has predestined us to be as Sons.

2nd Corinthians 3:18 says, *"So all of us who have had that veil removed can see and reflect the glory of the Lord. And the Lord--who is the Spirit--makes us more and more like him as we are changed into his glorious image."* We are not to remain the same. We are to go from glory to glory. In every season of our lives, we are to come out looking more and more like Jesus, not like ourselves. This is the true process of a human-*being*. We are to always strive to become more and more like Jesus, to be changed and transformed into His image and likeness.

*

The Greek word for son is *"huous"* which means someone who walks in the same tune of his Father as a son. It's someone who has the same nature and character as his Father; in quality, in resemblance, in ability and in character. A *"huous"* is someone who not only walks, but manifests everywhere they go, just like Jesus did.

Being a Son is the highest status or rank of honor that God the Father desires for all of His children to attain, but only chooses to give it to those who, after receiving the truth and accepting Jesus Christ into their lives, have completely done away with their old lives and are committed, dedicated and have an innate desire to grow and become more and more like Jesus.

In the Jewish tradition, when a boy becomes 13 years old (12 years old for girls) they become responsible for observing the commandments under the Jewish Law. To initiate their coming of age, they usually have a celebration called the Bar (or Bat) Mitzvah. This ceremony signifies a boy becoming a man (or a child becoming a son).

There is a reason why God didn't just send Jesus into the world to immediately die for our sins. There is a reason why Jesus didn't just show up on earth and started performing miracles. There is a reason why His ministry began when He was 33 and not when He was 9. It's because He was not yet of age.

Galatians 4:4 says, *"But when the set time had fully come, God sent his Son, born of a woman, born under the law God sent him to buy freedom for us who were slaves to the law, so that he could adopt us as his very own children.*" Jesus was born of a woman, just as you and I, and when He was born He had to humble Himself under the law so that He could set us free from the law that we were bound to. He submitted himself as a Jew and to the spiritual principles that came with the Jewish law. Because Jesus submitted himself to this law, He had to completely empty Himself out —forsake all of His rights as a Son and re-learn Sonship. This is the greatest form of humility that the world will ever know. C.S Lewis has a famous quote that precisely depicts what this scripture is saying. It says, *"The Son of God became a man to enable men to become sons of God."* He gave up His robes for rags. He gave up His royal crown for a crown of thorns. He gave up His rights, so that we could get ours back.

The Bible doesn't record any miracles taken place or being performed by Jesus while he was still a boy. But it does say that at age twelve, He surrounded himself with teachers and mentors that were at the Temple (Read Luke 2:41-52) because He knew that He had to place Himself in a position to grow. Jesus knew that He had a purpose for coming to earth. He knew that He had a mandate to fulfill and He made sure that He surrounded Himself with the right people that would help get Him to where He needed to be. Because He remained in His Father's house and surrounded himself with the right people, the Bible says that *"He grew in wisdom and in stature and in favor with God and all the people."*(Luke 2:52). This is the Father's desire for all of His children.

Before you got saved, your identity was hidden. Now, the only way it can be restored is through love, through oneness, through having an intimate and genuine relationship with the Father. Matthew 3:14 says that, *"After his baptism, as Jesus came up out of the water, the heavens were opened and he saw the Spirit of God descending like a dove and settling on him."* Sonship takes place when the Holy Spirit awakens and renews your spirit. This is what happened to Jesus after He was baptized. His spirit was awakened, and He could now walk in His manifested nature as a Son. This was His own personal coming of age ceremony and also the prelude to His ministry on earth. The Jordan River was where the Holy Spirit *confirmed* Jesus' identity, but it was also where the Father placed His mantle on His Son and *affirmed* His identity.

4

THE BECOMING PROCESS

"Being confident of this, that he who began a good work in you will carry it on to completion until the day of Christ Jesus." – Philippians 1:6

Throughout the Gospels we see how Jesus proved and revealed His Sonship to the world and now God wants us to do the same. Sonship takes a lifetime to learn. It doesn't just happen in one particular season of your life and then that's it. It's a continual thing. It's a daily thing. In the same way your physical body doesn't stop growing, your spiritual body doesn't either. Every single hour of every minute of every second of every single day we are to continue to grow and mature into the image of the Firstborn Son, Jesus Christ. If He had to grow into Sonship then who are we, mere mortals, not to follow in His footsteps?

Paul prays a very encouraging prayer in Philippians 1:6. that says, *"Being confident of this, that he who began a good work in you will carry it on to completion until the day of Christ Jesus."* But what is this "good work" that he's talking about? It's the working of Sonship! It's the becoming process! He's praying that the work of becoming all that God has called you to be as a Son of God will be carried out in you until the day that Jesus Christ returns.

This is the ultimate goal for every believer—that at the end our lives, we appear before the Father face to face and He says ... "Wow, you look exactly like my Son Jesus!" and embraces us. This is the goal. This is why we are here. To be conformed into the image of our Big Bro Jesus.

Romans 8:29 says, *"For those God foreknew he also predestined to be conformed to the image of his Son, that he might be the firstborn among many brothers and sisters."* (NIV) The Firstborn Son being conformed (or formed/fashioned) in us so that He can transform us from the inside out is our destiny. So don't think that looking like Jesus is impossible. It's actually your destiny to look like Him. You were born to be a Son of God. You were born for this. Sonship is in your DNA. It's innate. You can't escape from it even if you wanted to. You can try to fight it, run from it, or even try to suppress it but the truest form of who God has predestined you to must be revealed. It has to.

When Jesus says, *"Be holy for I am holy"* (1st Peter 1:16) or *"Be perfect, therefore, as your heavenly Father is perfect."* (Matthew 5:48) He's not saying it to tease us, but to remind of us who are. By telling us He's commanding our destiny. He's commanding us to be who we were born to be. As a Son of God, you don't have to work to be holy or to be perfect. Holiness and perfection is us. It's who we are.

Holiness and perfection are indeed achievable. This world will tell you that nobody is perfect and that it's completely impossible to live a holy lifestyle. But if you date it back to the time where Adam and Eve were in the Garden of Eden, where everything was perfect and holy, you see how this is exactly how God intended for all of creation to be. What He intended back then, is the same thing that He intends for us right now.

The work of becoming and maturing into Sonship isn't an easy process. It takes hard work. It takes sacrifice. It takes diligence. It takes perseverance. And it also takes you being in a state of constant repentance, constant self-evaluation, constant pruning, constant cleansing and constant sanctification. If you are to be revealed to the world, if you want people to see

God's Son in you then you have to be comfortable with being uncomfortable. You must get to a place where you are able to be vulnerable before the Father and allow Him to work in every single area of your life. If not for your sake, then do it for the sake of those whose lives are dependent on your maturing.

Matthew 22:14 says, *"Many are called but few are chosen."* This means that *all* are called, but *few* choose to take heed to this call. Once you say yes to the call of God concerning your life, you are giving God permission to have His way in your life. So allow Him to prune you and to peel back those layers. Allow Him to break down those walls that you've built up. Allow Him to build your character, to mold and shape you into the man/woman of God that He has predestined you to be. Allow Him to carry those burdens that you've been holding onto for 10 years. Just allow Him because there is nothing but good that will come out of it.

We go through Sonship in the same way that Jesus did. While on earth, Jesus experienced times of suffering, persecution and many trials and tribulations even up to the point where He was about to be crucified. Hebrews 2:18 says, *"Since he himself has gone through suffering and testing, he is able to help us when we are being tested."* So because Jesus has already gone through what we will experience now through Sonship, we have Him to look up to as our Big Brother to help us overcome.

The process of becoming a Son certainly doesn't happen overnight. But it is so worth it because after you've been tried through fire, you will come out looking just like your Elder Brother Jesus. (1st Peter 1:7 *"These trials will show that your faith is genuine. It is being tested as fire tests and purifies gold--though your faith is far more precious than mere gold. So when your faith remains strong through many trials, it will bring you much praise and glory and honor on the day when Jesus Christ is revealed to the whole world."*)

2nd Timothy 2:21 says that *"So if anyone cleanses himself of what is unfit, he will be a vessel for honor: sanctified, useful to the Master, and prepared for every good work."* All the pruning, the cleansing, the sanctification, the uprooting and the tearing down must happen before God can partner with you here on the earth. Get rid of all the pain and defects in your heart so the anointing that flows through you won't be short circuited. God seeks to use vessels of honor, those who have clean hands and pure hearts so that His glory can be displayed through us.

There is an African song that is sung in many Pentecostal African churches that says:

"You are the Lord, that is Your Name,

You will never share your glory with any-body,

You will never share your glory with any-body

Almighty God that is your name."

But in the African culture, this song has been sung countless of times out of context. When this song is usually being sung in African churches, we take it for its literal meaning that because God is Almighty, Omnipotent, All-Powerful, and Self-Suffienet He will never share what only belongs to Him. While in fact, this is partially true. God is definitely a Self-Sufficient God and doesn't need anyone's help at being God, the second part of this song is what's invalid. Hebrews 1:3 says, *"The Son is the radiance of God's glory and the exact representation of His nature."*

Yes, it's true! God doesn't share His glory with just *anyone*; He only shares it with His Sons. He shares it with those who have His spirit. He shares it with those He entrusts His Kingdom with.

In John 17:22, Jesus said, *"The glory that you have given me I have given to them, that they may be one even as we are one,"* What glory is Jesus talking about here? He's talking about God's own glory. The same glory that was spoken of in Hebrews 1:3 is the same glory that Jesus gives to us now. Jesus came to bring us back into this glory that we once shared with God at the very beginning. Hebrews 2:11 says, *"So now Jesus and the ones he makes holy have the same Father. That is why Jesus is not ashamed to call them his brothers and sisters."*

When Jesus came to earth and died for our sins, everything that was His now became ours too. Everything that Jesus inherited, we inherited too. We too, now have a place in the Kingdom of God. How awesome is it that Jesus is not ashamed of us, but that He calls us His brothers and sisters and shares what rightfully and fully belongs to Him with us. And because we get to share and partake in His glory, this is why we must also share in His sufferings.

FROM SLAVES TO SONS

When you give your life to Christ, your name gets written in the Lambs Book of Life, you become a citizen of Heaven and are seated with Christ in heavenly places! But soon after receiving salvation, we often wonder why some things in our lives are still the same; why we still have some bad habits and why our attitudes haven't completely shifted. Could this all be due to the fact that you may still be operating under a slavery mentality?

A slavery mentality is a way of thinking that was conceived when sin entered into the world. It shapes the way you view life, yourself and the people around you. People with a slavery mentality struggle with their relationship with the Lord because they are unable to comprehend the finished work of the

Cross. They struggle to understand how a holy and righteous God could ever love someone like them. They don't believe they are worthy of anything good in this world. They try to work for the Father's love, approval and acceptance. People operating in a slavery mentality are limited and restrained from growing up to their full potential as Sons.

We enter into our salvation still believing the lies that the enemy has been whispering in our ears since we were 3-years-old. Lies like: you're ugly, no one loves, you're not smart enough, you're gay, you're dumb, nobody loves you and you have no purpose. For some of you, it may even be because of what your parents have said about you, what your tradition or cultural beliefs say or even what the negative people that you associate yourself with has been saying that is keeping you bound to this mentality. Nevertheless, because of this you take these same lies and translate them into your new life as a believer and now there's this war going on in your mind that you're trying to fight in your strength.

Hence, it takes the working of the Holy Spirit through the process of Sonship to transform your mind and to get you to think like a Son. You literally have to take off that old slavery mentality and put on the mind of Christ daily because it's the mind of Christ that gets you to a place where you will start believing that you are everything that God says you are.

In 2nd Samuel 9:5-13 there is a story of how a slave named Mephibosheth became a son through the process of spiritual adoption. Now at this time, David was King over Israel and Mephibosheth was Jonathan's son and the last one alive of Saul's grandchildren because David killed all the other sons of Saul's house at the command of God. The slaughter of Saul's seven remaining sons was an act of strict justice. But…
"But the king spared Mephibosheth, the

son of Jonathan, the son of Saul, because of the Lord's oath that was between them, between David and Jonathan, the son of Saul. "(2nd Samuel 21:7)

David wanted to fulfill his promise to Jonathan by showing Mephibosheth kindness. David showed Mephibosheth kindness by giving him all of the property that once belong to His grandfather Saul and by permitting Him to eat at his royal table (2nd Samuel 9:7).

But because Mephibosheth had a slavery mentality, when David wanted to bring him into his royal courts, he responded by saying, *"Who is your servant, that you show such kindness to a dead dog like me?"(*1st Samuel 9:8) A response like this is only one that a slave would give. Mephibosheth spoke so lowly about himself because all he's ever known was that he was good for nothing. He saw himself as unworthy, dead beat, worthless and useless. No one has ever shown him kindness, love and compassion the way David did. No one ever has ever affirmed His identity. All his life, Mephibosheth has been a slave and the only way He knew how to respond to David's kindness was exactly how a slave would.

But David responds in verses 9-10 and says: *"Then the king summoned Saul's servant Ziba and said, "I have given your master's grandson everything that belonged to Saul and his family. You and your sons and servants are to farm the land for him to produce food for your master's household. But Mephibosheth, your master's grandson, will eat here at my table." (Ziba had fifteen sons and twenty servants.)."*

In these scriptures, we see how David disregards Mephibosheth's comment, not out of rudeness but out of urgency to prove to Mephibosheth that it wasn't some trick that he was trying to play on him (hence why the scripture says *"He summoned Ziba"*). When a king summons someone/something, it is a call to action. David wanted to prove his kindness to Mephibosheth by giving another servant his duties and giving him the right to eat at his table. But the story doesn't stop here, the scripture goes on and says, *"And from then on Mephibosheth ate regularly at David's table, like one of the kings own sons."* (Verse 11) *"And Mephibosheth, who was crippled in both feet, lived in Jerusalem and ate regularly at the king's table."* (Verse 13)

Would you look at that! Within the matter of a few minutes Mephibosheth goes from being a slave to a son! This is exactly what God does for us through Jesus!

In this story, we all represent Mephibosheth, Jonathan represents Jesus and King David represents God. We are all crippled, hopeless, lost, insecure, and *"dead dogs"* who needed a king to rescue us from ourselves, just like Mephibosheth. But it wasn't until God remembered the promise that He made to the prophets long ago that He was going to show us loving kindness by sending His Son in likeness of a man to die for us. God took us as slaves and adopted us as Sons and now we get a chance to eat and dine with Him in His kingdom for all of eternity! That's exactly what happened in this story; a crippled slave became a Son with inherited rights and privileges in the Kingdom. It wasn't because of anything that Mephibosheth did or didn't do. It wasn't because he deserved it or worked his way to eat at the King's table. No. It was simply because of the loving kindness of a King.

WHO IS A SON?

- **A son is someone who has rights and privileges.** (John 1:12 *"But to all who believed him and accepted him, he gave the right to become children of God."* Philippians 2:9 *"For you have been given the privilege of serving Christ, not only by* *believing in him, but also by suffering for him.")*

- **A son is someone who is an heir.** (Galatians 4:7 *"So you are no longer a slave, but a son; and since you are a son, God has made you also an heir.")*

- **A son is someone who has the inherited right to call God Father.** *(*Romans 8:15 *"The Spirit you received does not make you slaves, so that you live in fear again; rather, the Spirit you received brought about your adoption to sonship. And by him we cry, "Abba, Father.")*

Galatians 4:6-7 *"Because you are sons, God sent the Spirit of his Son into our hearts, the Spirit who calls out, "Abba, Father." So you are no longer a slave, but a* son; and since you are a son, God has made you also an heir."

- **A son is someone who has access to the Father at all times.** (Ephesians 2:18 *"For through Him we both have our access in one Spirit to the Father."*)

- **A son is someone who is free.** (John 8:36 *"For who the son sets free, is truly free indeed."*)

- **A son is someone who is confident in whom they are because of who He is.** (Proverbs 14:26 *"In the fear of the LORD there is strong confidence..."*)

- **A son is someone who is led by the spirit on all occasions.** (Romans 8:14 *"For those who are led by* the spirit of God are sons of God.")

- **A son is someone who is protected.** (Psalm 61:7 *"A thousand may fall at your side, ten thousand at your right hand, but it will not come near you."*)

- **A son is someone who is seated in heavenly places**. (Ephesians 2:6 *"...and raised us up with Him, and seated us with Him in the heavenly places in Christ Jesus,"*)

- **A son is someone whose citizenship is in Heaven.** (Philippians 3:20 *"But we are citizens of heaven, where the Lord Jesus Christ lives. And we are eagerly waiting for him to return as our Savior."*)

- **A son is someone who is someone who lacks nothing.** (Read Psalm 23)
- **A son is someone who constantly abides with the Father.**

I could literally go on and on and continue to list attributes of a Son and cross-reference them with scripture but that will be the end of this book. Love is foundational principle to Sonship and the most important thing that you can ever know as a Son is that you are perfectly loved by a perfect Father.

Many people will call this whole idea of becoming a Son of God blasphemous but as long as you are a slave, the idea of being a Son, or even hearing someone call themselves a "Son of God" will always seem so preposterous to you. Some will even believe that I am leaving women out of this whole equation because I fail to mention "daughter". Galatians 3:28 says,

"There is no longer Jew or Gentile, slave or free, male or female. For you are all one in Christ Jesus." So if you are in Christ, your race, nationality, age and even your gender doesn't matter because we are all one. We are all sons.

And the truth is that God wants us to start seeing ourselves as Sons because it's going to take many Sons revealing their Sonship to restore all of creation.

5

THE THREE GROANINGS

*"For we know that all creation has been groaning as
in the pains of childbirth right up to the present time." –
Romans 8:22 (NIV)*

Man was the king of creation under God.
He had dominion over the whole of creation.
Because of this his fall not only affected
Himself but the whole of creation as well.
When Adam sinned, creation fell right along
with him. Once sin entered into the world
restriction, bondage, decay, and evil influence
was released over creation. This means that
people could actual murder, have hatred in their

hearts towards their brother, people could engage in relations with the opposite sex, invoke evil spirits, practice idolatry and all sorts of other things that violate the Kingdom of Heaven.

This also means that every living thing is now subject to death, disease and decay— animals, birds, fish, flowers, trees. Everything that lives is contaminated to some degree. This why nothing in this world lasts forever and death exists. This is also why people find it so hard to believe in God's love. People don't seem to understand why a loving and just God could ever allow all this calamity in the world. But another thing that people don't understand is that what we see in the world today isn't a result of God turning his back on us, but a result of man turning our backs on Him.

In Romans Chapter 8, we see three different groaning's taking place: the groaning creation, the groaning of believers and the groaning of the spirit. All groaning, hoping and longing for the day when everything in this earth will pass away and return back to the original state in which God intended for it to be.

CREATION GROANS

Romans 8:20 says, *"Against its will, all creation was subjected to God's curse."* Remember when Adam sinned, God said in Genesis 3:17 *"Cursed is the ground because of you."* It is not creation's fault that it is cursed, it's man's fault. And because its man's fault and man is the offspring of Adam, it is man's job to restore creation back to its original glory. But it is not the sons of Adam that will restore creation back; it is the Sons of God that will.

We often say things like: "There is so much evil in this world" and "This world is so perverted" and we are so quick to point fingers at each other, when, in fact we should be pointing to ourselves. We caused it. We did it. It's all our fault. The world is evil because we made it to be evil. The world is perverted because we made it to be perverted. Now it is time for us to own up to our mistakes and get together to solve the problem.

All of creation is in such agony and pain right now and we are not even aware of it. Romans 8:22 says, *"For we know that the whole creation has been groaning together in the pains of childbirth until now."*

We witness creation groaning when we see natural disasters like hurricanes, earthquakes and tsunamis completely destroying millions of hospitals, schools, businesses and homes. We witness creation groaning in the fluctuating weather patterns. We witness creation groaning when we hear about terrorist's attacks and nations going to war with each other and kingdoms rising up against kingdoms (Matthew 24:7).

We also witness creation groaning when we look into the eyes of animals and see the hurt and pain in their eyes. They know that they were meant to live in a world where there was no pain, no suffering and where people would actually care about their existence. We see it in plants as well, how in one season they are beautiful and flourishing and in the next, we trample on them as if they have no significance.

When man fell, they fell too.

No one cares about the polar bears that are extinct. No one cares enough to water the beautiful flowers that are shriveling to death. No one cares about the little girl that is dying in the hospital due to leukemia. No one cares about the millions of men, women and children that die every year due to a hunger-related disease. No one causes how bad poverty is plaguing many third-world countries.

No one cares enough to pick up the liter on the sidewalk pavement. No one even cares about their brother who is hungry. We complain about all these things, but we don't care enough to do anything about. It's crazy how we seem to care absolutely nothing about the world's problems when we are the ones who caused it. Just take a look around you and you will see that everything in creation has a deep knowing that something is wrong with the universe.

Romans 8:21 says, *"But with eager hope, creation looks forward to the day when it will join God's children [sons] in glorious freedom from death and decay!"* All suffering is temporary and creation knows that. Just like a woman experiencing birth pains, the sufferings of the moment are passing away by the joy that is coming ahead. Creation has been in pain since the fall of man. Since the fall of man it has been enduring in pains but the birth pains that creation has been experiencing will soon come to an end. It is only a matter of time.

Jesus molded a lifestyle here on earth that compels us to follow suit. Romans 8:19 says, *"For the earnest expectation of the creation eagerly waits for the revealing of the sons of God."* (NKJV) Notice how this scripture doesn't say that all of creation is waiting for the revealing of *the* Son of God, but *of* the sons of God. Why? Because Jesus Christ (The Firstborn Son of God) already came to earth, revealed who He was in His nature and character of the Father and fulfilled the mandate that was given to Him by His Father. After dying on the cross, resurrecting on the third day and right before He ascended into Heaven to reclaim His throne, He left us with our own mandate. For this very reason, we cannot remain stagnant in our growth, we must follow after this Son of Man, this Nazarene that beautifully demonstrated what it meant to be a Son of God on earth and to have genuine relationship with the Father.

In the life of every believer, there needs to come to a point where you move past the rudimentary teachings of Christianity because all of creation is eagerly waiting for the Son in you to be revealed, not the child.

Everything in creation is waiting for you to become everything that you were created to be. Creation knows who you are. It knows how powerful you are, it knows that you are God's crowning achievement and it knows that you hold the key to setting it free from its death and decay.

There is a groaning in creation for you to know who you are because there is a revelation that needs to be revealed and that revelation is you.

THE BELIEVERS GROAN

Just like creation, we who have been saved by grace through faith and are being led by the Spirit, also suffer and groan. Our groaning is due to the present corruption and futility we see both in ourselves and in this world we live in. The anticipation while waiting for the day where we are free from our present state of suffering and what we shall become someday as fully matured Sons is what intensifies our groaning. Romans 8:23 says, *"And not only this, but also we ourselves, having the first fruits of the Spirit, even we ourselves groan within ourselves, waiting eagerly for our adoption as sons, the redemption of our body."* We cannot wait until the day that we are completely free from this world and our fleshly bodies and get to see Jesus face to face and share in His glory forever. But what we need to understand is that *"If we are to share in his glory, we must also share in his sufferings"* (Romans 8:17).

SHARING IN THE SUFFERINGS OF CHRIST

Often times as believers God will put us through many different challenging experiences, many different trials and tribulations for the sake and freedom of others. God seeks to partner with His Sons in His vineyard but before we can partner with Him, we need to be tried, we need to be tested, and we must to suffer. After all, if we don't go through sufferings then how can the fullness of Christ become perfected in us? 1st Peter 4:13-15 says, *"Dear friends, do not be surprised at the fiery trials you are going through, as if something strange were happening to you.*

Instead, be very glad—for these trials make you partners with Christ in his sufferings, so that you will have the wonderful joy of seeing his glory when it is revealed to all the world." In verse 13, Paul tells us not be to be surprised when we go through these many different trials. Instead, we should expect them to happen in the same way that Christ did.

We don't like broken bones, we don't like pain, we don't like wounds, cuts or bruises. We don't like anything that will take us out of our comfort zones. We like our comfort, we like our reputational statuses, we like wealth, we like prosperity. We seek for contentment, for enjoyment, for fulfillment and for satisfaction. But in order to fully reign in Christ, we must be able to go through, grow through and withstand the trying times. We must be able to forsake our comfort for discomfort.

In 2nd Corinthians 11:23-27, Paul shares with us the many trials that he has faced all in the name of Christ.

"...I have worked harder, been put in prison more often, been whipped times without number, and faced death again and again. [24]

Five different times the Jewish leaders gave me thirty-nine lashes. [25] Three times I was beaten with rods. Once I was stoned. Three times I was shipwrecked. Once I spent a whole night and a day adrift at sea. [26] I have traveled on many long journeys. I have faced danger from rivers and from robbers. I have faced danger from my own people, the Jews, as well as from the Gentiles. I have faced danger in the cities, in the deserts, and on the seas. And I have faced danger from men who claim to be believers but are not. [27] I have worked hard and long, enduring many sleepless nights. I have been hungry and thirsty and have often gone without food. I have shivered in the cold, without enough clothing to keep me warm."

Paul understood that his present sufferings were putting him on the path to future glory. He knew that every night he went hungry, every lash and whip that he took was setting him up for the glory that awaits him. Paul understood that in order to reign with Christ later, suffering must take place now. Paul says in Acts 14:22, *"Through many tribulations we must enter the kingdom."* And Jesus said, *"If they persecuted*

me, they will persecute you." (John 15:20)
Now, persecution isn't always going to look
like you being taken away to a far away desert
to be be-headed. Persecution can look like you
being mocked and made fun of for sharing the
Gospel in your work place. It can look like you
being ridiculed for living a life that follows
after the lifestyle of Jesus. It can look like you
being shunned for not conforming to the ways
of this world. It can also look like you being the
only person in your family who is a Christian.

As believers, we must be prepared to suffer
for the name of Christ. You may wonder, "But
if God is such a good and loving Father then
why would He want any of his children to
suffer?" To answer this presumed question,
because the Father desires for His children to
mature, he made suffering a prerequisite for
Sonship. Suffering is what produces maturity.
Suffering is what shapes and molds your
character. Suffering is what builds you up and
helps you gain spiritual muscle. Suffering not
only tests your faith but it increases it as well.
Suffering keeps you humble and always brings
you crawling to the Father. It allows you to

know be in a constant state of recognizing that you are nothing without Him. Suffering is essential in the life of every believer because it was essential in the life of Jesus.

1st Peter 2:21-24 says:

"²¹ For God called you to do good, even if it means suffering, just as Christ suffered for you. He is your example, and you must follow in his footsteps. 22He never sinned, nor ever deceived anyone.

²³He did not retaliate when he was insulted, nor threaten revenge when he suffered.

He left his cause in the hands of God, who always judges fairly.

²⁴He personally carried our sins so that we can be dead to sin and live for what is right."

Think about all the experiences in your life that were painful, the times where you had to suffer (whether it be physically or emotionally) and compare those times to where you are now. I think you and I can both agree that it is safe to say that if you did not go through those trying times then you wouldn't be where you are today. Let's equate this example to Jesus. If

Jesus wasn't bruised for our iniquities, crushed for our sins; if the punishment that brought us peace wasn't laid upon Him then we would not be here today.

In the moment, suffering isn't easy. It's painful and it hurts. There are times where you feel like the whole world is against you and you want to resort to giving up and throwing in the towel just like Jesus when He was praying to the Father on the Mount Olives. Luke 22:42-44 says, *"⁴²Father, if you are willing, please take this cup of suffering away from me. Yet I want your will to be done, not mine." ⁴³ Then an angel from heaven appeared and strengthened him. ⁴⁴ He prayed more fervently, and he was in such agony of spirit that his sweat fell to the ground like great drops of blood."*

This was a very humble moment for Jesus. Jesus was at His crux. He had reached His climax. At the Mount of Olives, His cup of suffering was completely full and He was at His breaking point. Jesus was about to bear the weight of sin of all of humanity on His back and He was in so much pain and agony to the point where He began sweating blood. He knew that He was about to be betrayed, arrested and taken into the hands of Pontus Pilate for doing absolutely nothing other than claiming that He was the Son of God.

But Jesus pressed through because more than He wanted His cup of suffering to be taken from Him, He wanted the Father's will to be done. So Jesus submitted to the Father's will and *"he prayed more fervently"* for strength. Jesus Christ had to go through much suffering all for our sake and now, it is our turn to suffer for His. This is the reason. We suffer because the Son suffered.

Although there are many benefits that come with the package of being a Son of God, we must not forget that we are not immune to the sufferings of this world. We live in a world that we are not from but just like any alien of any foreign country, we have to adapt. This is why we still fall sick and why we are still affected by our economy whether we like it or not.

We as believers groan because of all of the present sufferings. We groan because we long to go home. We groan because we want to be fully delivered from our present situation. We groan because we know that there is hope. Romans 8:24 says, *"²⁴ For in hope we have been saved, but hope that is seen is not hope; for why does one also hope for what he sees? ²⁵ But if we hope for what we do not see, with perseverance we wait eagerly for it."*

This hope that we don't see but oh so anticipate for is what causes us to persevere through our present sufferings.

THE SPIRIT GROANS

In the same way that all of creation groans, waiting for the revealing of the Sons of God, in the same way that we as believers groan, waiting for our own day when we fully mature into Sonship, so the Holy Spirit also groans.

The Holy Spirit is the power of God on the earth. He is who Jesus Christ left us with before He went to be reunited with the Father in Heaven. He is our Friend, our Advocate, our Helper, our Counselor and everything else that you could ever need Him to be in this fallen world. The Holy Spirit gets it more than any other. He understands the depth and the gravity of our sufferings as believers that's why He helps us in our areas of weakness. In 2nd Corinthians 12:9-10 Paul says, "But he said to me, *"My grace is sufficient for you, for my power is made perfect in weakness." Therefore I will boast all the more gladly about my weaknesses, so that Christ's power may rest on me. That is why, for Christ's sake, I delight in weaknesses, in insults, in hardships, in persecutions, in difficulties. For when I am weak, then I am strong."* It is when we are weak that the power of the Holy Spirit can be made perfect in us. This is why Paul boasts and delights in his weakness because they essentially make him strong. Paul understood that he had the Holy Spirit to make intercession for him.

The Holy Spirit is intimately involved in the agonizing reality of the encumbrance of the weight of sin in the lives of those in whom He lives in. He unites with our desire to be free from the flesh and from the corruption of this world to receive our full Sonship and to be completely perfected in Christ. Our eternal glory is secured by the groaning prayers (or intercession) of the Holy Spirit.

Romans 8:26 says *"And the Holy Spirit helps us in our weakness. For example, we don't know what God wants us to pray for. But the Holy Spirit prays for us with groanings that cannot be expressed in words."* We do not know what to exactly pray for in this time so the Holy Spirit takes on our weakness and prays for us.

Have you ever been in a time of prayer where you were praying in the spirit (otherwise known as speaking in tongues) and you begin to let out cries from the depths of your stomach? Then the next thing you know you start pouring tears and you don't even know why. You don't even know what's going on but you recognize that it is the power of the Holy Spirit that is at work within you. When we cannot speak, the Spirit speaks for us to God. He is the one that pleads for us, the one that groans for us to be revealed. He is communicative link between our hearts and the heart of God the Father.

THE PRESENT GLORY

The word "groan" means "to make a deep sound because of pain or some strong emotion".

So here we have creation groaning, the believers groaning and the Holy Spirit groaning. These three groaning's take place all because we are eagerly waiting for the hope of future glory. We are waiting for the world that Jesus promised us, a world that is free and devoid of sin.

But this better world can happen now. This new world can happen now. There is something inside of creation that wants to partake in this glory right now. Colossians 1:27 says that *"Christ in us is the hope of glory"*, meaning that Christ being formed and conformed in us is the hope of the glory that we want to see in this world right now! It's Jesus. He is the hope. He is the restoration. It's the Son in us that this world wants to see. Yes, there is a future glory that awaits us all when Christ returns, but there is also a present glory that needs to take place here and now.

Isaiah 60: 1-2 says, *"Arise, shine; for your light has come, and the glory of the LORD has risen upon you. For behold, darkness will cover the earth and deep darkness the peoples; But the LORD will rise upon you and His glory will appear upon you."* This is a prophetic declaration that is speaking to the Sons of God. For the Sons of God, there is a glory inside of us that yearns to be revealed. As darkness is covering the earth, the Sons of God will also rise up and take their rightful stance in this world and reveal the glory (which is Christ) to all of creation.

6

THE FATHER WANTS TO REVEAL

YOU

"Again Jesus said, "Peace be with you! As the
Father has sent me, I am sending you."
– John 20:219 (NLT)

The missing element in all of mankind is the realization of what a father is like. Many people in this world are suffering from daddy issues and it all can be linked to many different reasons. For some, it may be abandonment, mistreatment or even abuse that you have experienced from your natural father. For others it may be that your father has always been present in your life but you never really felt a true connection with him. Due to one of these reasons or another, your heart is now wounded and you are now left with growing seeds of anger, bitterness, unforgiveness and insecurity in your heart. As a result, you begin searching everywhere in this world trying to fill the void of your father not being there for you at your third grade recital when all the other kids parents were or of him sexually abusing you between the ages of 5 and 8.

So many people walk around this world trying to fill voids in their hearts that only the Father was meant to fill. Many women sell themselves to men to make a living and you know why they do it? It's because they don't know that they have a perfect Father who loves them.

John 8:1-11 tells a story about a woman who was caught in the act of adultery on the Mount of Olives. Verse 9 says, *"When the accusers heard this, they slipped away one by one until Jesus was left in the middle of the crowd with the woman."* This scripture right here paint a picture of a beautiful Father-daughter moment.

Jesus waited to be alone with the woman to talk to her because what she needed was the closeness and the familiarity of a Father. She was lacking the love of the Father and Jesus wanted to present to her this love. So Jesus says in verses 10-11, *"10Where are your accusers? Didn't even one of them condemn you? 11"No Lord," she said. And Jesus said, "Neither do I, Go and sin no more."* Jesus didn't stone her nor did He condemn her. He just restored her identity back to her and affirmed that she was a beautiful daughter that is loved by a perfect Father.

The lack of a father's love, protection, affirmation and presence are all number one causes of identity issues. Deep down inside all we really want is to be loved. All we really want to is to hear "I'm so proud of you" and "You are so beautiful". All we every really wanted was to sit on our daddy's lap.

THE DESIRE OF THE FATHER

Jesus came to reveal to this world what the

Father is like. He came to reveal the Father's heart towards you. He came to reveal His love and compassion towards you. He came to reveal your identity. Jesus came to reveal the Father because this is what the world was missing, this is what the worlds was lacking— perfect love from a perfect Father. No one before Jesus revealed the Father. Not David, not Abraham, not Isaac or any other prophet. It was Jesus and it could have only been Jesus because He and the Father are one.

To reveal something means to "lift the veil". So when the Father reveals something it's not in that moment that He creates it because the thing is already there. He just unveils it and makes it seeable. This is what the Father seeks and desires to do with all of His kids. He wants to reveal us to the world. He wants to show us off but before you can be revealed to this world, you need to know who you are and the only way you can come to know who you are is by knowing who the Father is.

Knowing the Father comes through having an intimate and genuine relationship with Him. This was the "secret" to Jesus' life; that everything that He did on earth was a result of the Father working through Him.

God is a perfect Father and He has perfect kids. He is so much bigger than what you could ever think or imagine. He desires the very best life for your life and for you to live up to your maximum potential as His Son. But again, none of this can happen outside of relationship with Him. Having a relationship with God is a necessity to becoming all that He has called and created you to be. It is not an option and there is no other alternative. It has to begin with relationship.

The Father has called all of His kids to evolve, to grow and to mature into the image and likeness of His Son. He has called us to rise on wings like eagles and soar. He desires for you to go from chickens to eagles, from infants to sons. He doesn't desire to see you stay in the same place that were in last year, last month, last week or even yesterday! He wants to take you higher and higher! He is calling you to live in a different realm, a realm that requires you to leave what you have ever known behind.

There is something in the heart of the Father

that seeks for us to partner and co-labor with Him in the earth. There are legions and legions of angels that exist but God chose His answer to restore creation to be a in the form of a man, a Son. He intentionally created man with desires so that we can turn them into dreams and those dreams into living realities to impact the re-construction of all of creation.

When you begin to walk into your identity as a Son of God you will begin to see what God sees, do what He does and can take all of the amazing gifts and talents that He has placed inside you and submit it at the feet of Jesus and allow Him to glorify Himself through them.

GOD RAISE US UP

Whenever God wanted to do something in the earth, he had to raise up a Son. He rose up Joseph to preserve the land of Egypt from a severe famine. (Genesis 45:5-7). He rose up Moses to bring the people of Israel out of Egypt (Exodus 3:10). And He rose up Jesus to give His life as a ransom for many (Mark 10:45). This whole idea of God raising up Sons is nothing new. God has been in the business of raising up Sons to perform signs and wonders throughout the world since ancient times.

Someone else's life is dependent on your maturing and on your revealing. The salvation, freedom and redemption of many is dependent is dependent on you becoming all that God has called you to be. God created you for this world and this world needs you to be the best you that you can be. This world cannot do with a faulty version or carbon copy of you. It needs the real you; the you that God placed inside your mother's womb. God is calling you to come and claim the inheritance that has been set before you as a Son of God so that you can begin walking in your true identity.

*

There is something special about this generation that God wants to do through us. But before we can do it, we have to allow Him to raise us up! We have to allow Him to mature us, to hone us, to mold and shape us. We have to allow Him so that we can be prepared once He sends us out.

There is about to be a massive shift in this generation. The Lord is about to raise up a generation of people who will indisputably and undeniably begin to walk on earth exactly how Jesus Christ did. He is raising up a generation of people who will boldly stand in the gap for Him; people who will walk in the fullness of who God has predestined them to be without limitation or restraint. This group of people, namely, the Sons of God, will completely annihilate the spirit of mediocrity and mundanity that has grown rampant within the body of Christ.

The Lord is saying that enough is enough. It's time for the church to arise in power! No more shallow Christianity. We have to grow pas being content with living the "normal everyday Christian lifestyle". It is time for the bride of Christ to mature! It is time for the world to know that God has a people who are called by His name; a chosen people, a royal priesthood, a holy nation—Sons that He wants to send out to liberate creation from the bondage of corruption and bring them into glorious freedom!

There are so many gifts, talents, visions, future business and ideas that God has deposited inside of you; not for you to keep to yourself but to bring about the betterment of the world. We have been sleeping on our destinies, our callings and our purposes! We have kept them under-locks and have grown to become a people who, ironically, settle for nothing more than less. Less than what God has called and created us t be. We cannot continue to do this world a disservice by settling! Beloved, it is time to for us to wake up! We have to stop playing with our destinies because the state of this world is at hand.

God wants Israel back. He wants America back. He wants Africa back. He wants Asia back. He wants England back. He wants the world back! But before He can reach these countries and the continents, before He can reach the states and the cities, before He can reach your communities and your homes, He has to reach you; He has to raise you up. It starts from you. The answer to what the world needs is inside of you!

REFERENCES